THE
PROSPEROUS
COACH

Increase income and impact
for you *and* your clients

Praise for *The Prosperous Coach*

"A must-read for every coach. Rich Litvin and Steve Chandler offer a revolutionary approach to creating a career and business that you love. No internet marketing. No email list. Just one great relationship at a time."

Marci Shimoff, #1 New York Times best-selling author of *Love for No Reason* and *Happy for No Reason*

• • •

"The sad truth of the coaching industry is that many of the most caring people give up after a time because they can't make enough money to survive and thrive. Steve Chandler and Rich Litvin are on a mission to give every coach the chance to succeed on their own terms, and they do it with a directness and humor that makes learning fun. I've hired them to teach on a number of my programs, and even after twenty-two years in the business I always take away at least one new thing to increase my own impact and income!"

Michael Neill, founder of Supercoach Academy and author of *The Inside-Out Revolution: The Only Thing You Need to Know to Change Your Life Forever*

• • •

"*The Prosperous Coach* grabs you by the collar in Chapter One and doesn't let go. My heart is still racing. This is one of the most direct, bold, and provocative books I've ever read. You are doing your clients a disservice if you don't finish it and act upon it immediately."

Derek Sivers, founder of CD Baby and author of *Anything You Want*

• • •

"Since research shows the happiest people in the world are those who help others, it must mean coaching is the happiest profession! With infectious enthusiasm, Steve & Rich show you how to thrive so you'll not only have a financially rewarding career but also a wonderfully enjoyable one. Coaching sure beats working for a living!"

David Meerman Scott, best-selling author of *The New Rules of Marketing and PR,* now in over 25 languages from Bulgarian to Vietnamese

● ● ●

"Rich Litvin and Steve Chandler are business thought leaders who count. They shatter the myth that you can't create wealth whilst making a big impact on people's lives. *The Prosperous Coach* will help you create a new story that when you and your clients find joy, meaning and emotional connection you can feel inspired and make money."

Chip Conley, founder of Joie de Vivre Hotels and author of *Peak*

● ● ●

"Becoming a Master Coach and having a lucrative coaching business is not a mystery. Building a mid- six or seven figure coaching practice occurs through service-oriented actions on a consistent basis. Chandler's coaching catapulted me to a seven-figure coach and I coach the world's most powerful business leaders. In *The Prosperous Coach,* Litvin and Chandler take the smoke and mirrors out of building a lucrative consultancy and make it practical. Read this book, share it, and apply it."

Stephen McGhee, leadership consultant and author of *Climb to Freedom*

● ● ●

"There are tons of books out there that can teach you marketing tactics and sales strategies. But once in a while a book comes along which gets you to focus on what really matters—human relationships! *The Prosperous Coach* is one of those rare gems which inspires, challenges, and allows for no excuses. Its contrarian approach may yet change your business and your life for the better. Grab a copy now!"

Shama Kabani, best-selling author of *The Zen of Social Media Marketing*

"Coaches, if you buy only one book to launch or enhance your coaching business, make it *The Prosperous Coach*. Litvin and Chandler throw conventional wisdom to the wind—no marketing, no email, no fancy business card. Just step-by-step proven methods to create a successful business with high-paying clients. Once I started reading, I couldn't put this book down. When's the last time you said that about a business book?"

Laurie Lawson, CEC, PCC, Past President, International Coaching Federation-NYC, Executive Producer, *Coach World TV* and *Coach Chat Radio*

• • •

"In *The Prosperous Coach* seasoned pros Rich Litvin and Steve Chandler reveal the secrets that have catapulted them and their clients to outrageous success. I loved reading it. If you are curious about the world of coaching, read this book. If you are a coach, devour this book; do what it says, and prosper."

Mandy Evans, author of *Emotional Options: A Handbook for Happiness* and *Traveling Free: How to Recover from the Past*

• • •

"Rich and Steve have written a fantastic field guide for creating a successful coaching practice. This book is full of hard-won insights and practical distinctions. Whether you already have a thriving practice or have been struggling to find clients until now there are gems here for you."

Jamie Smart, author of *Clarity: Clear Mind, Better Performance, Bigger Results*

• • •

"*The Prosperous Coach* should be mandatory reading for anyone considering a coaching career or joining a coaching program. Litvin and Chandler strike the right balance between teaching you how to be the best possible coach and teaching you how to make money doing it. It's a comprehensive study of the way any coach needs to build and maintain client relationships. This book is a 'hell yes!'"

Bryan Franklin, Top 1% Executive Coach, California Leadership

• • •

"Litvin is a rare breed: a world-class coach who is also an expert at understanding the business of coaching. After reading and applying the strategies in *The Prosperous Coach*, you will be, too. Become a 'fearless coach.' Litvin will show you how."

Dr. Sean C. Stephenson, author of *Get Off Your BUT: How to end self-sabotage and stand up for yourself*

• • •

"As someone who has been coaching for a long time, I wish *The Prosperous Coach* had existed when I was learning. It would have saved me so much time and energy. Whether you are a new coach or an experienced coach who is ready to get to the next level, I highly recommend you read this book if you wish to achieve prosperity as a coach."

Sophie Chiche, founder and curator of lifebyme.com

• • •

"This is a unique book—a manifesto for a new kind of coaching. I have clients today because I applied the principles and disciplines outlined in these pages. It's the most useful and practical book on coaching I've read."

Chris Morris, Coach

• • •

"I find this to be one of Chandler's most powerful books. For coaches or prospective coaches: I encourage you to read and be coachable in your listening to this book. Go beyond knowledge and engage in the material for your own transformative learning; become the coach you desire in your own self-coaching. Find the answers within you. Connect, convey, and create!"

Rob Owen, Vice President of Global Information Services at Microchip Technology Inc. and adjunct Professor of Operations Management at Thunderbird School of Global Management

• • •

"If I drop this pen, I know what will happen. It will fall. That's the law of gravity at work. We get that. What Chandler and Litvin get is the law of crushing it as a coach. You practice these disciplines—you crush it. Period."

Chris Dorris, Personal Transformation Coach

• • •

"*The Prosperous Coach* is full of such powerful insights that struck me as I read it—again and again and again. In fact, I literally just walked out of an event I'd paid a sizable four figures to attend because of one of the insights that Rich and Steve share. There are many excellent tips in this book. They are laid out simply and clearly and, most importantly, they are actionable. If you follow them, not only will they make your coaching practice more successful, but your life full of ease, spaciousness, and freedom."

Rachel Rofe, best-selling author and founder of *Never Have A Bad Day Again*

• • •

"This is a book for anyone who wants to enroll high-performing clients. It will teach you to build deep confidence in yourself, boldly request fees that reflect the value of your clients' dreams, and build a serious business. Chandler and Litvin's unorthodox approach will challenge you, amuse you and help you demolish the myth that business has to be hard."

Stever Robbins, Executive Coach and top-10 business podcaster

• • •

"This book will shake you up. It will challenge you. But if you open your mind and lean into the teachings, it has the potential to transform your coaching as well as your bottom line. This is far more than a book about making more money. It is about creating vastly more meaning, value, beauty, and happiness in yourself and the world. But beware, there are no magic bullets here. You will have to show up and serve boldly in order to get the results they promise. And why wouldn't you?"

Molly Gordon, Master Certified Coach

• • •

"What a fresh and unique approach Steve Chandler and Rich Litvin bring to the coaching world! The insights, tips and strategies they share will transform the business (and life) of any coach who puts them into practice. I am totally inspired by this book!"

Karen A. Cappello, PCC, BCC, Coach Mentor and Coach Trainer

• • •

"*The Prosperous Coach* rocked my world by throwing out of the window everything I thought I should be doing to market myself as a coach. It offered me great relief to know that there was an effortless path to creating high-end clients. Talk about counterintuitive, Litvin and Chandler take the focus off the busywork of marketing and put it back on pure connection with the client, where it belongs. Read this book, do what they tell you, and a prosperous coaching practice is inevitable."

Mindie Kniss, Coach

"Right now you're wondering whether reading this book will make a positive and noticeable difference in your life. It absolutely will. You're right on the precipice of transforming not only your life, but the lives of all your clients. And you're about to learn from two of the masters. If you're ready for success and prosperity while fulfilling your mission to help others, you're reading the right book."

Erin Pavlina, Intuitive Counselor and Master Intuition Consultant

• • •

"*The Prosperous Coach* is an action-oriented wake up call to consultants. If you really want to have high-performing, high-paying clients, it's time to stop hiding behind social media and your computer screen. It's time to engage with real people. Litvin and Chandler will show you how."

Jeffrey Hayzlett, Global Business Celebrity and best-selling author of *The Mirror Test*

• • •

"Steve Chandler is one of the best authors of our time. In *The Prosperous Coach* he teams up with Rich Litvin to create yet another masterpiece that is needed in the Coaching industry. If you want to succeed at coaching the right way this book is a must read."

Gary Henson, author of *Strategies to Future Proof Your Business* and president and founder of BusinessCoach.com

• • •

"In this remarkable book, Steve and Rich get right to the heart of what it takes to beat the odds and become a successful, prosperous, purpose-driven coach. If you truly want to build your practice, then read this book and practice what it preaches."

Brian Whetten, Ph.D., M.A., founder of Selling By Giving

• • •

"Chandler and Litvin are rapidly acquiring international guru status in the professional coaching world. By implementing the potent content of this extraordinarily good book, backed by your own commitment, your future as a prosperous coach is assured."

Dusan Djukich, innovator of Straight-Line Coaching and the best-selling author of *Straight-Line Leadership: Tools for Living with Velocity and Power in Turbulent Times*

• • •

"Any coach, consultant or service provider who is sincere in her desire to make a difference in the world while making a good living will immediately digest this book and keep it close. No matter where you are in your practice (just beginning or thriving), this book holds the key to catapulting you to your next level of success. Chandler and Litvin invite all of us to step forward with a magnificent combination of fierceness and love."

Michelle Abend Bauman, J.D., M.A.

THE
PROSPEROUS
COACH

Increase income and impact
for you *and* your clients

STEVE
CHANDLER

RICH
LITVIN

MAURICE BASSETT

books for athletes of the mind

The Prosperous Coach: Increase Income & Impact for You and Your Clients

Copyright © 2013 by Steve Chandler and Rich Litvin

Contact the publisher:
Maurice Bassett
P.O. Box 839
Anna Maria, FL 34216-0839
www.MauriceBassett.com
MauriceBassett@gmail.com

Contact the authors:
www.SteveChandler.com
www.RichLitvin.com

Editing by Chris Nelson
Cover designed with love by Peleg Top
Book layout by Danielle Baird
Illustrations by David Michael Moore

ISBN-13: 978-1-60025-030-9

Library of Congress Control Number: 2013934199

First Edition

To you, the coach.

—*Steve*

I dedicate this book to my dad. You taught me to believe half in what I see and nothing in what I hear. You had no idea what a gift this would be to me as a coach.

I love you, Dad.

—*Rich*

Table of Contents

Fearless Coaching

Deep Inner Work

Appendices: Creating an extraordinary coaching practice

You are not alone

It's lonely at the top.
Ninety-nine percent of people
in the world are convinced they
can't do great things,
so they aim for mediocre.

—Tim Ferriss

Overcome the notion
that you must be regular.
It robs you of the chance
to be extraordinary.

—Uta Hagen

The tiny, versatile hummingbird symbolizes the message of this book.

A hummingbird's wings beat up to eighty times per second. They can rotate in a complete circle, allowing it to hover in mid-air, fly forwards, backwards, up, down, sideways and even upside-down.

The laws of physics say it should be impossible for the hummingbird to fly.

Clearly nobody told the hummingbird.

We dedicate this book to those of you who are ready to do the impossible.

THE
PROSPEROUS
COACH

CHAPTER 1

"Why isn't this working?"

by Rich

It was seven in the morning. It was grey and cloudy outside and it felt almost as grey and cloudy in my room as I hunched over my computer, tired and frustrated. I had been working so hard over the past year to build my skills as a coach. I had done training after training, and I knew my coaching was powerful. Yet as I peered at my bank website in the early morning light there was no arguing with the cold, hard facts of the numbers. I had almost no money left in my account.

What I wanted to scream was, "Why? Why? Why isn't this working?"

And I was angry because I'd just received a clear *no* to the bold request I had sent to a coach named Steve Chandler. You see, Steve had a reputation for helping coaches become prosperous. Some of the most successful and world-class coaches I knew had trained with him.

So I had emailed Steve with an extraordinary offer. I had written, "Steve, I cannot afford to attend your Coaching Prosperity School. But if you let me attend for free, I will pay you double by the end of the program."

Excited by my offer, I was crestfallen to receive his reply: "Rich, I want you to be the coach who can create the money first."

My chest was constricted and my breathing short, because signing up for Steve's school would drain the very last of my savings. And yet a sensation deep inside of me knew: "You have got to do this."

I wrote the check then and there and walked to the mailbox with my heart beating fast in my chest. I wanted to commit. I wanted to play full out—for the first time in my life. I dropped my check in the mail and a couple of weeks later I met Steve in person for the first time as I became a member of his Coaching Prosperity School.

The numbers don't lie. It was just two months later when I realized I had already made *ten times* my investment in my own coaching. For the first time in my coaching life I had found a way to look into the eyes of a potential client and have them smile as they said the magic words, "How do I pay you?"

As I write these words today I have a deep sense of inner confidence about my ability to create prosperity as a coach. I no longer use my bank account as a way to make myself feel bad (or good). And I know how to create the income and clients that support a lifestyle I love.

I attended the Coaching Prosperity School four times in total. I eventually became a faculty member and began to lead seminars alongside Steve.

I have learned to thrive as a coach. And in this book, alongside my coach, mentor and now good friend, Steve and I get to share our world with you.

● ● ●

A coach once asked me, "What's the secret to being an extraordinary coach?"

"Extraordinary clients," I replied.

"That's easy to say," he retorted, "but how do you get extraordinary clients?"

What I said to that coach is what I will now say to you: Be *fearless* in your coaching. And be *fearless* in how you create clients.

Show your clients what they cannot see.

Say to your clients what no one else would dare to say.

And you will have all the clients you ever desire.

This book will show you how. It provides you with access to the world of the prosperous coach. It will help you increase your impact and your income—and do the same for your clients.

The scene is set in the next section of the book, called *The Miracle of Coaching*. You will choose your level of engagement and learn to set a high bar for yourself and your clients. Not many coaches are willing to play such a high-level game, so you will find yourself in the rare air of the world's best coaches.

In *Creating Clients* you will learn effortless and powerful ways to sign clients you love while maintaining your integrity. There are no gimmicks or manipulative techniques. You will develop a system that works for you, building deep, meaningful connections that lead to referrals and clients, time after time.

In *Fearless Coaching* you will explore the two levels of fear that coaches face. There is the fear within your coaching which is often expressed as people-pleasing instead of powerful service. And then there is the fear of "selling" and enrolling clients that typically results in never making bold, life-changing proposals and having only uncommitted clients.

In *Deep Inner Work*, you will examine—and move beyond—the deep-seated beliefs that hold most coaches back from success for themselves and their clients.

Finally, the Appendix distills the essence of the book into a set of tools you can use to begin creating your own clients immediately.

This book is for coaches who want to match their skills and talents with the committed clients they serve.

It is for coaches who are ready to be world-class.

Every time you coach you change the world.

CHAPTER 2

Without a client you're not a coach

by Steve

I HAD BEEN RUNNING MY Coaching Prosperity School for years, with remarkable results. Students learned to sell their services at levels they never thought possible. My school was the only coaching school that didn't teach you how to coach. It focused all its time and energy on only one thing: acquiring your next client.

My own life was completely turned around by coaching, and like a mad scientist who has found a cure for cancer I wanted to give that turnaround back. So I began coaching coaches on how to build prosperous practices.

Because a coach without a client is not a coach. I know. I have been there. And how did that sorry state get cured? By my own coach, the ultimate coach, Steve Hardison. Now I want to give coaches everywhere what he gave me.

It's not enough for coaches to simply be good coaches.

If you are a coach reading this book I want to make you as good an enroller as you are a coach. For your client's sake and for the sake of humanity itself. Coaching can only help civilization if there are clients.

No one has been coached as I have, and now all I have is yours.

I started my Coaching Prosperity Schools because there was one thing missing in our profession, and it was the most important thing of all: a coach's ability to build a client list. A coach's mastery of the client-acquisition process. It was missing.

Coaches were all gung-ho about learning to be great coaches. They went to schools, read books, listened to powerful audios, got certifications, even got coaches who taught them to coach better. But the big missing was still missing. How do I get a client? How do I sell without being afraid?

Sales fear. Call reluctance. Money fear. Confusion of service with personal worthiness. All diseases inside the coaching profession. Many times these diseases were fatal. Coaches gave up.

One brilliant coach I know gave up and started selling cars. The Centers for Disease Control (actually what I call the "victim centers" known as coaching associations) put out bleak and troubling statistics about how the average coach was making less than minimum wage. A stunning thing.

Meanwhile the coaches in my school were reporting weekly billings of three-, five- and often more than ten-thousand dollars. One coach in the most recent school reported a fifty-thousand dollar week. And one of my school graduates now routinely earns seven figures a year coaching, although when he came to me four years ago he could not make himself sell.

I think my best student ever was Rich Litvin.

He was a brilliant coach. In my school he was dazzling in the way he could interact with other coaches. In mere minutes he could change their view of the world from one based on fear to one full of possibility. The only thing missing in Rich's life was income.

Once he got the hang of what this book will teach you, he soared! Soon he was teaching others how to succeed. Clients—and he had a lot of them—raved about him. They were high-paying clients, too. Soon Rich and I were doing seminars together. It wasn't long before I was actually learning from him. When he got up to talk in our seminars, I never left the room. I just got my notebook out and learned.

Now it's your turn.

Show your clients
what they cannot see.

Say to your clients
what no one else
would dare to say.

And you will have all
the clients you ever
desire.

THE
MIRACLE OF
COACHING

CHAPTER 3

To hell with circumstances

by Rich

To hell with circumstances. I create opportunities.

—Bruce Lee

I HAVE A CAREER THAT DOESN'T even make sense. The only way I can describe it is to say this: I am in the miracle business.

People spend time with me. We talk. And miracles occur.

One of my clients is a mother of three. When I first met her she was feeling completely stuck because she had this "crazy" dream of a certain famous billionaire entrepreneur writing the forward to her book and becoming president of her charitable organization.

But she didn't know him, and she knew he would have no reason to meet with a stranger, let alone agree to her requests. She kept saying to herself, "Am I just dreaming too big? Am I pushing too far beyond what is possible?"

She sat down with me and began to share her dreams. And we began to meet, week after week. She immersed herself in our coaching. Some days she would show up disappointed and low in energy as these dreams seemed so far out of reach. And some days she would show up full of a sense of possibility as she took steps further and further outside of her comfort zone.

Within a few months she had a meeting on her calendar between herself and the billionaire. She showed up to the meeting alert and focused, her whole body trembling with energy. But she stayed connected with her bigger purpose, and by the end of their meeting he had agreed to both of her requests. And soon after he flew her out to California to meet Oprah.

* * *

An Olympic athlete I coached was struggling with her blocks around money. The voice in her head would say, "You're supposed to be a world-class athlete. So why can't you raise any funds? You're a loser." She was so hard on herself because she lived with the daily frustration of selling calendars in a seemingly hopeless attempt to fund her Olympic bid. She was a beautiful woman and the calendars had stunning photos of her, but at seventeen dollars apiece she was going to need to sell a whole lot of them to get to the Olympics.

When we met, I dived deep into what she was doing all of this for. After a few minutes she began to cry. With tears rolling down her cheeks, she admitted that this was for something so much bigger than her. She had a dream of creating a foundation that would teach children that everyone was capable of Olympic-sized feats. As she finished speaking, she looked up into my eyes—and her own eyes were sparkling.

I told her to tell the world about her mission. I told her to take all the focus off herself and to place a singular focus on sharing her mission with the world.

Within twenty-four hours after this single coaching session with me she called to say that she had raised $40,000 of corporate sponsorship. I was thrilled. But I wasn't surprised!

* * *

A new coach wanted my help getting coaching clients. He had a background in medical sales and he was confused because his experience in selling seemed to be irrelevant to signing the kind of high-end clients he wanted to coach. In fact, he had made just $15,000 in his first year as a coach.

He had explored creating websites and membership programs and search engine optimization and building an email list, but none of that was working for him. What he was saying to himself, almost daily, was, "When is this marketing approach ever going to work for me the way all the experts say it should?"

We spent time together and I shared with him everything that we teach in this book. He devoured what I taught like it was information that would transform his life. And then he did something that not everyone can do with powerful information. He applied it.

He invested in becoming my Apprentice and dived in deep. He worked with me closely, week after week, for a full year. In the course of that year, his second ever as a coach, he faced many challenges, but he stayed in the game and soon began to enroll his first high-performing clients. His own clients began to have great successes, and by word of mouth alone he filled his practice. By the end of his second-ever year as a coach he had billed $400,000 in coaching fees.

• • •

In my work with coaches, consultants or even small business owners, I have developed a reputation for doing one thing exceptionally well. My clients create a thriving practice—by invitation and referral only.

So, although I say I am in the miracle business, what I actually do is help my clients see their world differently. Because when you help someone see their world differently, their world changes.

When someone sees the world differently, they show up differently, and they create results that looked impossible a moment before. That is a miracle.

CHAPTER 4

Drop the phony stuff

by Steve

I LIKE TO COACH PEOPLE WITH radical and provocative metaphors. I use them to wake people up to what's possible when they are willing to connect with another person.

Most coaches waste time communicating without really making a meaningful connection.

One of the coaches in a prior school I ran had an $18,000 month. She used to have months that were closer to $3,000, but one way she improved her billings was by ruling out lunch, dinner and "coffee" as options for that first meeting with a coaching prospect.

Those options are from 1950s' sales books that say you should first get to know someone socially.

But the truth is that it actually diminishes the chances you'll land a coaching client if you have lunch with them first and establish your relationship as a social one.

What do you do instead?

Throw them in the slammer.

Get a small room in a tin warehouse by the waterfront with a single lightbulb hanging from a frayed wire in the ceiling and one small table and two metal chairs and go full Mossad on them.

Or whatever your version of that would be.

But you must create a clearing in which transformation has a chance to happen.

If you just "have lunch" they will never feel the value of coaching. They'll just think you are an amiable, affable, social person who is fun to chat with—but why pay big bucks for that?

Most of the mistakes failed coaches make are of the information-manipulation variety. Lots of marketing and social media posting. Lots of learning about branding and niches. Lots of trying to win friends and influence people. None of it works. Ever. In the world of coaching.

Because coaching changes lives. Therefore all the shallow people-pleasing forms of sales manipulation are inappropriate. In fact, they are off-putting. But this is actually good news for most of us who hate that activity anyway.

Coaching is a good profession for people who are genuinely devoted to making a difference in the lives of others.

Coaching is not a good profession for friendship-seeking frauds and phonies. What is most sad to us is to see a genuine, good, authentic person spend their day trying in vain to market and sell and manipulate people into their coaching practice because "That's how I thought it was supposed to work."

That is not how it works. We will show you how it works.

The coaching profession has a problem that is two fold: there is a low bar for entry and a high bar for success.

CHAPTER 5

Set your bar high. And clear it.

by Rich

THE COACHING PROFESSION HAS a problem that is two-fold: there is a low bar for entry and a high bar for success.

The barrier to entry for coaching is now SO low that literally anyone can become a coach. There are companies that will certify you for free, and almost every "coach training company" promises immediate wealth and success if you will just sign up for their coach training.

This means that many people experience coaching at the lowest end of the skill spectrum. Coaches who have trained online, coaches who have done a weekend workshop, and coaches who have simply read a book about coaching are hanging out their shingles and offering free sessions to tempt potential clients.

It's no wonder that despite the incredible results that real coaching can generate for clients, many people will have a poor experience of coaching.

But you don't have to be one of those coaches. You can be extraordinary if you are willing to put in the time, educate yourself, and turn pro. Use that high bar for success to your advantage. Be one of the committed coaches willing to clear that bar.

CHAPTER 6

Choose your level of engagement

by Steve

WE HAVE WORKED THROUGH THE YEARS with many coaches who have entered our seminars and schools, or who have studied the art of coaching with us.

We know from experience that all these coaches will end up as one of three distinct practitioners:

1. Pro coach

2. Part-time coach

3. Personal Growth coach

A Pro coach makes her primary living through coaching. And it is a good living—with a yearly income comparable to the income of other professionals in private practice (lawyers, doctors, accountants, etc.).

A Part-time coach is professional in the sense that he charges a good, strong fee for his work, but he has another primary vocation or source of income that sustains him, and he therefore does not rely on coaching for his livelihood. He simply has clients on the side.

A Personal Growth coach has received training in the profession and "knows how to coach," but does not do so professionally. Their skills still remain valuable tools for whatever work they do, especially in leadership roles, because good coaching always brings out the best in another person and can be applied almost everywhere people interact.

None of these levels is better or more honorable than another.

We've trained many coaches who have created a great living from their coaching income. Some now make high six- and even seven-figure incomes as coaches.

Several coaches from the Coaching Prosperity School have discovered the joy of coaching part-time. One went back to his first career as a computer programmer, another sold real estate and another led travel adventures around the world. They created an income with their day jobs that freed them from any neediness around signing clients. From that place, they were able to create a wonderful second income doing what they love.

A woman in our first Coaching Prosperity School, years ago, fully intended to leave her company and go out on her own as a coach. But in the course of acquiring the enrollment skills at the school and applying them inside her existing company she was offered a major promotion into a senior leadership position. She loved it and never looked back. She remains today, happily, at the Private level of coaching.

For a coach to fully turn Pro, a lot of time and energy must be invested in achieving a mastery level of effectiveness. For coaches there is no law school or medical school to force them into a Pro. They must take it upon themselves to self-educate and make the journey.

But that's the fun part. So hang on and see where this takes you.

Your clients are paying for their dreams.

And their dreams are priceless.

CHAPTER 7

Or be a struggling coach

by Rich

Not understanding the three levels of engagement will result in one thing only: a Struggling coach.

A coach who says they want clients but have few or none. A coach who says they want a six-figure income but who is afraid to charge for coaching. A coach who wants to coach clients but has never been bold enough to invest in their own coaching.

Learn to understand and apply the distinctions in this book and you will never be a Struggling coach.

Here are some powerful contrasts and distinctions that we see between Struggling coaches and those Pro, Part-time, and Personal Growth coaches who are thriving:

The Struggling coach wants to coach anyone and everyone. They are afraid to ask for money. They want to wait until everything is perfect before they charge for coaching. They spend their time, energy and money on "getting the word out." They think that marketing is essential in order to sign clients.

The Pro coach is committed to coaching, no matter what. Failure doesn't stop them. They are not embarrassed by their mistakes. There's no turning back.

The Part-time coach learns to love their full-time job. It's what brings in the cash to allow them to do the coaching they love in their spare time.

The Personal Growth coach loves coach trainings and reading and seminars as ways to deepen their understanding of life, business, money, health and relationships.

● ● ●

The Struggling coach thinks that because they give advice to their friends they will be successful as a coach. They coach without permission—friends, family and colleagues—and they cannot distinguish between impactful coaching and unsolicited advice.

The Pro coach learns to love selling coaching. And they know that cash is not the only way to be paid for coaching. You can be paid in experiences. You can be paid in relationships. You can be paid in learning. You can be paid in referrals.

The Part-time coach understands that limitation creates value. Only having a couple of hours a week for coaching makes them more attractive as a coach, not less.

The Personal Growth coach learns to love supporting their friends and family (with their full permission).

● ● ●

The Struggling coach thinks getting clients is the "hard" part. They seek more and more information about how to "get" clients. They want more and more information on the latest, newest "magic marketing system." And they think that they just need to find a guru to teach them the "right" way.

The Pro coach knows there is no "hard" part. They love the business side of coaching as much as they love coaching.

● ● ●

The Struggling coach tries to please everyone.

The Pro coach serves people and does not try to please them.

● ● ●

The Struggling coach wants to be comfortable. They want to be liked. They people-please. And they wonder why their clients miss sessions and don't show up on time.

The Pro coach knows that being uncomfortable is the only way to grow. And because they create such powerful agreements, their clients never miss or are late for a session.

● ● ●

The Struggling coach has huge dreams that overwhelm them.

The Pro coach has huge dreams, and takes tiny steps every day.

● ● ●

The Struggling coach is scared to ask for money or to state bold fees because they are afraid of rejection.

The Pro coach knows there is no such thing as a high-paying client. Your fees are just a filter for the clients you'd love to coach.

● ● ●

The Struggling coach spends their time creating a beautiful website, stunning business cards, requesting "likes" for their Facebook group and sends out tweets on the hour.

The Pro coaches their butt off.

* * *

The Struggling coach has never invested in their own coach. They don't see the message this sends, that they don't even believe in coaching enough to invest in it for themselves.

The Pro coach understands that receiving coaching is part of their professional development. They model the power of coaching by devoting a significant part of their time, energy, focus and income to being coached by the best coaches they know.

* * *

The Struggling coach thinks money is like oxygen.

The Pro coach knows that money is just money.

* * *

The Struggling coach thinks confidence is a *requirement* before taking action.

The Pro coach knows that confidence is a *result* of taking action.

* * *

The Struggling coach tries to sell the *concept* of coaching.

The Pro coach sells by giving people a powerful *experience* of coaching.

* * *

The Struggling coach seeks more and more credentials.

The Pro coach knows that credentials are irrelevant because the only question clients ever want an answer to is: *Can you help me?*

* * *

The Struggling coach is reactive.

The Pro coach is creative.

Safety is the enemy of success.

Be proud of your mistakes. Take a risk. Fail spectacularly.

And then go out and fail more.

CHAPTER 8

Love the "hard" part

by Rich

THE BIGGEST PROBLEM MOST COACHES face is that they think they are entitled to a career. "I'm a really good coach. Therefore I should be able to succeed as a coach."

The problem is that only fifty percent of becoming a successful coach is about your coaching.

It's the other fifty percent that will determine whether you thrive or even survive as a coach. The other fifty percent of what you need to do to become a prosperous coach is what we call Creating Clients.

Others call this "Getting Clients" or even worse, "Attracting Clients." And most coaches call this the "hard" part.

But as long as it remains the "hard" part you are not going to succeed.

Our motive in writing this book is to have you *love* this part of your coaching practice. Our dream is to have you master the art of creating clients. Our dream is for you to make the "hard" part easy.

Imagine two boxes. The box on the left is what you *do*. The box on the right is the *business* of what you do. The business of what you do includes sales and accounting and making proposals and bookkeeping and paying taxes.

Most coaches **LOVE** the box on the left

and they **HATE** the box on the right.

Most coaches put all their attention on the box on the left. They do more and more coach training. They invest more and more money in becoming a better and better coach. They *love* this box and spend money, time and energy over here.

But they *detest* the box on the right. They hate the *business* of coaching. To them it means selling and asking for money.

If you want to be successful you need to learn to love the business of coaching as much as you love coaching itself. And the simplest way to do this is to make the box on the right as similar to the box on the left as possible.

The moment I began to slow down my initial conversations with potential clients, my life changed. I didn't realize it at the time but I was learning to love the business of coaching. Now, I'll never meet with

the business
of coaching

the amount
of fun & success
you'll have as
a coach

coaching

The more these boxes overlap, the more fun you have and the more you thrive as a coach.

a potential client for less than two hours. And all I ever do to "sell" is to create a powerful coaching experience. So for me there's no more selling, there's just coaching, which I love. There *is* no "hard" part.

My business plan has become one line: *Meet fun and interesting people.* My attention is on building relationships and coaching people and making bold proposals.

I enroll my clients by coaching them. As simple as that. In fact, my calendar now has only two colors: red and blue. Blue signifies any time I am coaching a client. Red signifies any time I am creating a client. I have made the two boxes overlap so much that if you were to observe me on a coaching day you would be hard pressed to know whether I was speaking to a client or creating one.

Lead powerfully.

Challenge how your clients see the world.

They do not need sympathy. They do not need you to be their friend.

CHAPTER 9

Design your preferred lifestyle

by Rich

I don't know any other lifestyle. I get up in the morning

and I really do feel that the world is my oyster. I start that way,

the same as I would if I were preparing to write a song:

put a blank piece of paper up on the piano and go for it.

—Lesley Gore

M OST COACHES GIVE NO TIME TO considering the lifestyle they would love to have. Three years into a new career they discover that they are working longer hours than before they became self-employed.

A client of mine asked me to coach her as she transitioned from corporate work into consulting as a philanthropic advisor. The first thing we did together was to "create" her lifestyle. She told me she wanted to make Fridays the day she spends with her five-year-old son. In her previous job she had worked six to seven days a week and she was determined to never do that again.

So I had her block out every Friday in her calendar with the label "Meeting with Executive Board." (Nobody would ever know that her Executive Board consisted of just one person: her beautiful baby boy.)

She turned down her very first job offer of $350,000 for six months of consulting with a Fortune 500 company because they wanted her to work on Fridays, the very day she had chosen to spend with her young son. She called me in a panic and said, "What have I done, Rich?!"

I helped her to stay calm and to consider the impact of going back to her previous life of ninety-hour weeks with no time at all for her child—and so she held firm. She laughed out loud when a day later the company called her back to meet her terms.

Me, I love to travel. As I designed my own lifestyle, I got clear that I would need to coach my clients by phone in order to have the freedom to travel as much as I wanted. And I love to spend time in beautiful places, so when I do meet clients in person, we meet in beautiful hotels or in inspiring locations.

If you don't consider your dream lifestyle when you begin coaching, you become like the American executive who, in an old joke, arrives on a beach on a beautiful island.

The executive strolls down to the beach and notices a fisherman rowing in to shore. His boat is chock full of fish, and the executive asks him what he's doing.

The fisherman replies, "I've been fishing because I love it. And now I'm going to have a barbecue on the beach with my friends. I'll play guitar and sing and hang out on the beach, and then in the evening I will dine with my wife under the stars."

"That's crazy," says the executive. "You've caught so many fish! I can invest in you and we'll sell the fish and make a ton of money!"

"Why would I want to do that?" says the fisherman.

"Well, in a few months, we could invest the profits and buy a bigger boat and make even more money," says the executive.

"Why would I want to do that?" says the fisherman.

"Well, in a few years, we could invest the profits and open a factory on the beach and process our own fish and make even more money," says the executive.

"Why would I want to do that?" says the fisherman.

"Well, with all the profits from that you could eventually retire early. And then you could go fishing just because you love it. And then you could have a barbecue on the beach with your friends. And you could play guitar and sing and hang out on the beach. And then in the evening dine with your wife under the stars..."

Start to outline your dream lifestyle now.

Don't worry if it seems out of reach. Imagine your life five years from now. Ten years. Who are your dream clients? Where would you love to be coaching them? What else would you love to be doing?

People pay you not what **they** decide your coaching is worth, but what **you** decide your coaching is worth.

CHAPTER 10

Cultivate deep foundations

by Rich

STANDING AT THE FRONT OF the Fairmont Miramar Hotel in Santa Monica is a magnificent fig tree that has welcomed visitors from around the world for more than a century.

The tree is stunning, at over 80 feet in height and with a breathtaking 167-foot spread of branches.

I love to take clients to the hotel at the beginning of a coaching program. We sit on a bench that looks directly out at the tree, and the view is awe-inspiring.

I take time to point out the remarkably thick roots that in many places protrude well above ground. You cannot see the majority of the extensive and deep root system supporting the tree from *beneath* the ground. This is a wonderful metaphor for how a strong and deep foundation is needed for us to achieve great things in life.

To become highly successful as a coach, you need to master three disciplines:

1. You need to master the business of **Creating Clients** (in fact, to be highly successful, you need to *love* creating clients as much as you love coaching clients).

2. You need to become adept at **Fearless Coaching** (a willingness to courageously lead your clients in the most powerful way possible).

3. And beyond these, you need to be willing to work your own process—and do the **Deep Inner Work** necessary—so you can see your own blind spots. You can't take your clients any deeper than you have been able to go in your own life.

CREATING
CLIENTS

CHAPTER 11

Clients are created not attracted

by Rich

The best way to predict the future is to create it.

—Peter Drucker

YOU DON'T GET CLIENTS. You don't *acquire* clients. And you definitely don't *attract* clients.

Clients are created.

"Getting" clients is an old-fashioned, hunter-gatherer approach to growing a coaching practice. It's outdated because it puts all of your success in the hands of other people. It puts you in an aggressive mindset that isn't conducive to having people say *yes*. And it has your clients on edge, waiting for that moment when you are about to manipulate them.

"Attracting" clients has become a trendy phrase. But it's such a passive approach to growing a coaching practice. Having a powerful vision for your business is a fantastic idea. But no successful business was ever developed from creating a vision board and then sitting down and waiting for dream clients to knock at the door.

There is another way. A better way. And it occurs when you bring your creativity to the table. When you are willing to combine imagination with action.

The kind of clients you would love to work with are only created in a conversation. And high-performing, high-paying clients are only created in impactful, life-changing coaching conversations.

CHAPTER 12

Invitation and referral only

by Rich

If you enter a market and don't know what to do,
watch what everyone else is doing, and then do the opposite, if you
want to be successful. The majority is almost always wrong.

—**Earl Nightingale**

COACHES AND CONSULTANTS come to me when they are ready to create a practice with just a few high-performing, high-paying clients a year. At the beginning they are a little shocked to learn the following:

1. They don't have to use any traditional "marketing."

2. They don't need to create a "pipeline" to fill.

3. They don't need a website or a business card.

4. They don't have to go to networking events.

And their business *grows* by invitation and referral only.

My clients create a lifestyle they love with the freedom to do what is most important to them. Some of them may enjoy playing with internet marketing and social media. Many do not. The point is they don't *have* to.

Because the formula that Steve and I teach—and use—does not involve marketing.

It's a formula designed to build a relationship.

Not even relationships, plural—just *one* relationship at a time. Honoring the individuality of the person in front of you.

These days, I coach three days a week and I have a marketing budget of zero dollars. I have five one-on-one clients. I take two months of vacation a year and I coach mainly by phone, which gives me the freedom to travel anywhere in the world.

But life wasn't always like that.

For much of my working life I was a teacher. I was an employee working for others, working long, long hours for a paycheck that never changed—unless I sought promotion. Which I did regularly. Only to discover that often the more I earned, the less I was able to do what I really loved.

Fortunately, it turned out, one day a new boss arrived who wanted her own leadership team. And because I was one of the most recent hires, I was let go.

But soon I was using some of the coaching skills I had learned as an educational leader. Later I became a full-time coach and I trained with some of the world's best coaches. I became better and better at coaching.

Yet I earned just $4,500 in my first year as a coach.

Something wasn't working. So I hired a marketing expert. And a Search Engine Optimization expert.

And I earned just $22,500 in my second year as a coach. And I hated the boring marketing tasks that I was required to do.

So I began to do things differently. I fired the marketing "experts" and I began to take an old-fashioned approach. I put my attention on people and relationships instead of money and "attracting" clients. And everything began to change.

The popularity of social media had somehow made me forget that it's *all* about relationships.

My great-grandparents were refugees from Eastern Europe. They built a clothing store in Waterloo Station in London, England, about eighty years ago. They didn't have the internet or email or Google Adwords. If you came into their store they got to know you. They asked interested questions and they learned what you liked and what you didn't like. They took down your details. And if some clothing item you might like came into the store, they contacted you.

Great businesses have always known that the magic is in building great relationships.

Coaching is no different. And for you and your career, that is very good news.

Get a coach.

Because you can't take a client any deeper than you have gone yourself.

CHAPTER 13

Okay, here we go, a bold promise: THIS WILL GET YOU CLIENTS

by Steve

WE CALL THESE THE Eighteen Fearless Disciplines, because they are activities that work (but only when practiced).

Remember that you have to practice them, not just understand them. Not just agree with them. Not just appreciate them. Practice them.

They are not theories we always knew would work. They are retroactively collected practices harvested from *what has worked* for me and Rich and our clients over the years, and what still works today.

We'll describe them briefly first, then explain further in the next chapter.

1. **Sell the experience, not the concept,** so that the client's only decision is whether or not to *continue* coaching with you.

2. **No cold calling.** Use or *create* inner circle connections.

3. **Know the half-life of enthusiasm.** Act quickly.

4. **Do not use email** (for persuasion or confrontation) in the act of client acquisition when phone or in-person options are available.

5. **Use conversations.** Schedule conversations. Fill the day with conversations until your client list is full.

6. **Use certainty versus belief.** Speak from what you are certain of. Keep a success list.

7. **Share stories and case histories** versus features and benefits.

8. **Find the goal behind the client's goal.** Ask about your client's clients.

9. **Needy is creepy.** Stay with *their wants* versus *your needs*.

10. **The Lamp Post Metaphor,** from Michael Neill: Be the first and only totally committed *listener* in their lives.

11. **Maintain innocence in getting your yes/no.** *Yes* lives in the land of *no*. If they have to "go think about it" the conversation was not complete.

12. **Leadership in the close.** Direct all the action.

13. **Slow down.** All the wealth you want is right there in the next conversation. Don't have a huge to-do list, just be with Who's Next.

14. **Get a coach.** A coach without a coach is like a doctor who won't see a doctor. Get a coach who will build your practice and change your professional life.

15. **Leave the conversation in a context of possibility,** *not* a context of affordability.

16. **Limitation creates value.** Make sure you are the one doing the auditioning of the client, and not the other way around.

17. **Be constantly aware of role reversal.** Do not surrender your power, leadership and role as *the coach* in the conversation.

18. **Be great at what you do...not just good.** Have routines, habits and practices that guarantee that you become better and better as a coach every day. Read books, see movies, listen to audio and talk to people who make you better as a coach. Every day.

No high-performing client was ever created outside of a conversation.

And no high-paying client was ever created outside of a *powerful* conversation.

CHAPTER 14

Have the disciplines be fun

by Steve

THE DEGREE TO WHICH WE PRACTICE these disciplines is the degree to which our coaching practices grow in both revenue and clients.

Soon there is a movement toward really high-paying clients with good, strong fees for the coach. Those are our outcomes from practicing the disciplines.

Again, there's a reason we call them disciplines instead of other things like "tips" or "strategies" or "secrets" or things like that. Disciplines are activities that are practiced. Disciplines are things that you *put yourself through and work with* and take out into the world and *do*.

Soon they become activities you thrill to and breath in to. And when they are practiced out in the world with real people, they get amazing results. After awhile they are just automatic. They feel like natural acts of easy relationship-building.

Whereas these disciplines might have once been awkward and clumsy, they will become, if they are continuously practiced, *natural forms of self-expression.*

Take your time to really understand these disciplines so you can own them thoroughly and understand their value deeply. Slowly warm up to them and feel good about them. Soon you will get them at a DNA level.

Discipline #1: Sell the experience, not the concept.

The client's decision needs to be whether or not to continue with you. Coach your potential clients with all the impact and attention and time and energy and focus you'd give to your highest-paying client. Make their decision easy.

Discipline #2: No cold calling.

Use your inner circle connections. Cold calling is not necessary, ever, in the world of coaching or in getting clients. Calling people up cold when you don't know much about them and they don't know anything about you, and then trying to sell them something does not work with coaching. It's really a waste of time, and it's not necessary at all.

We're all connected. We can look each other up. We all know people who know you. We all have very few *degrees of separation* between us, and we can close these quickly.

Therefore, there are ways to prepare for my communication with a coaching prospect—even to over-prepare. I can rehearse really completely and make myself very knowledgeable about the person I'm about to talk to, which gets me eager to talk to them. No cold calling, please. You already know enough people who know people who know people. You really do, and if you slow your life down you'll see that.

Discipline #3: Know the half-life of enthusiasm.

Enthusiasm has a half-life. So if someone is excited about working with you, they have a certain measurable level of enthusiasm for your work and your coaching. Please know and see and experience the fact that this enthusiasm will fade over time—it has a half-life. And so, a week from now, it won't be as great and as strong and as vibrant as it is right now. No way to stop that deterioration of enthusiasm.

Yet most coaches are completely unaware of it! They worry and wonder why people aren't getting back to them. Even people who said they would!

My coach, the fabulous Steve Hardison, has taught me over the years (the last *fifteen* years) a distinction that he uses called *event-action*. I want to take my *action* as soon after the *event* as I possibly can.

Let's say someone has heard me speak to a group and they email me the day after and say, "Hey, I loved your talk, it was really great. I'm really interested in asking you about possible coaching." Now the enthusiasm is high! I don't want a lot of days to go by. I don't want a lot of time to pass because that enthusiasm will go down. It has to.

It does for anything in human life. Notice when you go to a concert and you love the concert and the next day you are telling everybody, "Boy, we saw Springsteen—it was amazing!" And then a week later you might talk about it a little bit, and a year later you're thinking, "Did I go to that concert?"

So enthusiasm goes through a half-life of continuous diminishment. However, if I can see that clearly, I can take advantage of that and make that play to my favor. I can always *act now*.

Discipline #4: Do not use email.

Now this is kind of an overstatement, because of course email has some effective uses. There are some things email can do for you, but most of the coaches I coach overuse it. They make the mistake of trying to use email for persuasion.

They try to use email to convince people of something or to get them to see the value of something. And it is ineffective that way. Because when people receive an email, quite often these days it's on their phone! As they step out of a meeting or as they get out of their car, they ask themselves, *"What can I delete quickly here? What do I have to respond to? What can I get rid of? I've got so much clutter coming in."*

Your email enters that crowd of messages. You don't want that. Coaching isn't appropriate for that kind of cluttered, frenzied world. Coaching is a very intimate experience, so you don't want to send a long email explaining the value of your coaching. It will not arrive in the same spirit in which it was sent. Please be awake to that.

So many of my clients in coaching have sent an email to a prospect who was considering the coaching, and it transpires that if they had only had a *conversation* something great would have happened. Instead they sent a long email, and now the recipient is considering the email. They read it, read half of it or... save it for deleting later. It's a good way to kill a relationship, especially in the world of coaching. So always look for the possibility of a conversation.

So that's **Discipline #5: Honor conversations.**

Use conversations, schedule conversations, have your day be about the next conversation you are going to have, because if you do that, you will get clients. All coaching agreements occur *inside* of a conversation. And no sale has ever occurred *outside* of a conversation.

If you can see this, you will have your *primary purpose* today to *be inside of a conversation* instead of pacing around, checking your email fifty times a day, handling family calls, writing a blog, wondering if you should write a book, going on social media, networking, trying some marketing—all those things we do that don't get us clients. All those things that eat up our whole day when we could have been in a conversation.

Discipline #6: Certainty versus belief.

Use certainty. That's your discipline. In other words, when speaking about what you do and the track record you have for coaching, use certainty. It improves your voice tone. Do not try to "believe in" yourself. Do not have selling be an emotional crisis about whether you are worthy of your fee. That will send you south. That will send you down the ladder. That will have you *not connect* with people.

The antidote to that is knowing what you are *certain* of. And then speaking with absolute certainty. "I just got off the phone with a client in London" is a statement of absolute fact. Keep at your fingertips things that are factually true about your work (and with a lot of beginning coaches I have them keep this list literally written out).

I don't need to "have confidence" or learn to believe in myself to say those *facts* to the person I am talking to. "One of my clients just had a 20% revenue increase last quarter."

When I fill my conversation with the things I am certain about—clients I have, work I have done, accomplishments they have achieved, I won't get nervous and I won't get scared. I want to really be connected with certainty. Because if I go the other direction—if I go in the direction of whether I am deeply, personally, really "worthy," then fear enters in.

Discipline #7: Share stories and case histories versus features and benefits.

Have case histories to tell. Have these things be stories you've told over and over and over. If somebody says, "Tell me how your coaching works," I might say, "Let me tell you about a woman named Mary Ann. She was struggling. She had various problems when she hired me. When we first sat down Mary Ann and I looked at her calendar..." So I'm telling this story and stories are beautiful because they connect with people and they end up saying, "Well, I have a situation similar to Mary Ann's," or, "I want you to do with me what you did with Mary Ann."

I once wrote a book with the brilliant Sam Beckford called *The Small Business Millionaire*. Both of us had been coaching all kinds of small business people for a number of years so we decided to write a story—a fictional story—of a coach who drives into town and saves a dysfunctional business from going under. The hero of the book is named Jonathan. We made up this story based on various coaching case histories. One day I got an email from a person who had read the book: "I want a Jonathan in my life. Will you call me?" So there's the power of stories right there. I ended up coaching that person for a year.

Discipline #8: Find the goal behind the client's goal.

As I'm speaking to my prospect and my prospect says, "I want to earn a million dollars this year," or, "I want my business to show a monthly profit," I don't want to just say, "Oh, okay, great. I'll help you do that! Let's put a coaching contract together. I've helped many people become profitable."

You don't want to go there yet. You want to find the goal *behind* the goal. "So tell me *why* you want your million. Let's say we've worked together for six months, and you are profitable now. How would that be a benefit to you? What options would you have that you don't have now? How would life be better?"

It doesn't have to be a business objective. If someone says, "I want to be able to communicate better with my ex-wife and my son, who lives with her," then you can look for the goal beneath that goal. "How would that make your life better? Let's count the ways."

The reason I'm asking these questions is that if I can find the goal behind the goal, my prospect is more connected to me than ever. Not only that, but sometimes we can create a shortcut. So, for example, my client might say, "Well, that would give me the time to really enjoy my life and be with my family more." And I might say, "What if we just created a life in which you were with your family more, and we also created the profit, but you didn't have to wait until you had a 200% profit increase to be with your family?"

There are so many wonderful things that can come up in an enrollment conversation when you find the goal behind the goal.

I don't want to be afraid to go negative either. Like Ron Wilder teaches in our live coaching school workshops, you *want* your client to describe the gap between the goal and today's reality. You want a long description of the client's *default future*: What if you don't do anything (like this coaching) and nothing changes? What does that life look like? What is the downside of this default future of yours? What are the consequences? How painful is it?

Discipline #9: Do not be needy.

You will have a hard time really hearing your client if your own mind is occupied by your own needs, as in, "I need this client, I need this money so badly, I really can't afford to lose this client, I'll discount, I'll do anything, I'll become desperate—I really need it."

If you've got this sense of extreme need in your mind, your behavior and your communication is going to push the person away. That's because neediness is creepy.

We don't want to be needy. We want to have it be the opposite. We want to talk and think deeply about the client's world, not ours. The sale always occurs inside the client's world.

If my client says, "Well, I'm going to think about this, I'll get back to you," I don't want to keep calling and emailing this person like I'm *needing* this work. Anything needy is creepy to the other person. Human need in the world of business is really off-putting. It causes people to not want to work with you. So it must be stopped.

Many times I have my clients who are coaches put on their computer the phrase "needy is creepy" just to remind them. Because look what people do. They check in, they touch base, they annoy people: "I'm just checking in. I'm just touching base. I'm just trying to find out if you are going to work with me. I'm just trying to find out if you are going to be my client," and that's really uncomfortable to another person.

We want to practice different ways to stay connected. We want to explore ways to deliver value in each communication. We practice these different approaches when we communicate because we'll get clients so much faster that way.

If you haven't heard back, send a gift and a note. Don't even refer to working together. Contribute and serve. You don't need them; they need you. Behave accordingly.

Discipline #10: The Lamp Post Metaphor.

This is something Michael Neill taught me. Any time I catch myself wondering if my coaching is really good enough to be charging what I charge—any slippage in my confidence, or my realization of how good coaching really is for people—I think about a lamp post.

The point Michael makes is that even talking to a *lamp post* would be good for a person. Let's say a person leaves his place of business every evening and walks over to a lamp post and speaks to it. Maybe he vents, maybe he talks about the problems of the day and about opportunities for tomorrow and areas where he can make improvements.

It's just a lamp post sitting there. But if he returned to that lamp post every evening and shared his successes and challenges of the day and his goals and dreams for the next day, even *that* would make his life better, would help create a better person. Even talking to a lamp post every evening would be beneficial to a person.

So your clients would get value if you just showed up. But as a coach you bring an entire world beyond a simple lamp post. You can really listen, you can see things. And you as a coach can be better than a lamp post. You can talk back.

Discipline #11: Maintain innocence in getting your yes and no.

Please know that *yes* lives in the land of *no*. Don't be afraid of *no*.

So, for example, when you are talking to a prospect, when people are talking to you about coaching and you really feel they've had a good experience of it and the conversation is about to come to an end, do not be afraid to live in the world of *yes* and *no*. Do not be afraid to ask an innocent question like, "Is this something you would like to do?"

Now notice how innocent that question is. It's not pushy, it's not salesy. Please see yourself in the same light as if you were a waiter in a restaurant. See yourself *serving* someone by asking that question. If you were a waiter in a restaurant you would come up to their table at the end of a meal and say, "Would you like coffee? Would you like dessert?" That's *service*. And if there's a *yes*, then you bring coffee, and if there's a *no* then you don't, and you don't care which. You're serving with your question.

A lot of times coaches don't see that. They think a question is pushy and salesy and puts pressure on a person. It doesn't—it serves. "Is this something you would like to do?"

And if a person says *no*, that person usually explains what's behind the *no*. "No, because…" Whatever is behind the *no* is showing me where a *yes* could come from if we keep talking. So *no* is fine, *yes* is even better. But the implied "maybe someday" does not serve either one of you.

Discipline #12: Show leadership in your enrollment conversation.

In sales training they call the agreement phase of the conversation "the close." Most coaches refuse to *direct the action* during the close. They go soft and vague and the next thing you know the client has left the conversation and nothing is on the calendar and no money is in the mail. This happens because of lack of direction.

Let's say someone says, "Yeah, I really want to do this coaching," and you say, "Okay, hey great, so I'll be getting back to you with a proposal and availability, and after that you'll get back to me, and after that we'll set it up…"

Now it has disappeared! And the client's life is happening and there are all kinds of new opportunities to spend this coaching fee elsewhere. A new granite countertop, for example, might be discussed over dinner.

And so coaching with you just sort of fades into the ether. Because they have second thoughts, or someone else is asking for money in their world and they are thinking, "Well, I could postpone the coaching."

I don't want the conversation to disappear into the ether. I'm the *coach* in this relationship so I want to show some *leadership*. I want to *direct the action* so that once someone says they want to work with me it gets completed!

"Okay, great, so if you want to do this work, and you're ready to begin, here's what you need to do. Open your calendar so we can put our first session on it. What's a good date and time for you? Wonderful. Now you can either pay at the website, mail your fee in or bring it to the first session, whichever way is most convenient for you. Any questions about that? Excellent. I look forward to this."

Now I'm directing the action as if you're coming to a great auditorium and I'm standing outside and I ask, "Do you have your tickets?" "Yes." "Okay, then please go into that line. Now, when you get into that line, you'll go here, then inside, and then talk to the usher; he'll seat you."

It is a great service to people to *direct* them. When someone wants your work—wants your coaching—please *direct them*. Don't get all shy and deferential because money is involved. It is not pushy to direct. It does not put pressure on a person. It really helps. People are asking to be coached. They are asking to be led at this point. They are asking to be directed.

Discipline #13: This discipline is really important. It's called **Slow Down.**
I've never had it *not* work to get people more business—to increase their revenue—when they just slow down.

Please look at who your next conversation is with. Who are you talking to? Who has emailed you in the last forty-eight hours? Slow everything down. Because everything you want is right here in front of you. You just don't see it because you're racing around.

You're racing from one meeting to another, from one quick conversation to a brief email, and you're skipping all over the place. You are not creating relationships. You're just "touching base."

Remember that coaching occurs because of long, slow conversations. It occurs because of the focus you give to someone. It occurs because they have a sense that you are there for them, that they are very important to you, that you have *time* for them. You cannot have that happen if you don't slow down. And the more you slow down, the more you'll get done in this profession.

I had a person in my Coaching Prosperity School and he was doing fairly well—I mean, compared to a lot of coaches. He was making a couple hundred thousand dollars a year, but he was racing all over the place and he was always frantic to get into his own future every day. He was like a fly buzzing against a window, trying to fly through the window getting into his own future. It doesn't work.

The coach I'm talking about always felt he was not doing enough. He needed to do more and more and more, and he thought that somehow more frantic activity and busyness would be the way to get his income up even higher.

Soon he found out that if he slowed down, life would get better. Especially in the income department. If he took *more* time off, and if he took long walks on the beach, his income would get bigger and his life would get simpler and better. It was a total revelation to him, and his income went from $200,000 to $600,000 in a period of about eight months. All from slowing down.

Discipline #14: Get a coach.

If you don't have a coach who is working with you, if you don't have that ongoing growth and continued improvement in your own world, if you do not believe in coaching enough to have a coach, how can you go to someone and tell them that coaching is vital?

It's really a total contradiction. Coaches tell me their biggest problem is that they don't have much income. And at the same time they're trying to sell their coaching based on the idea, "If you hire me as a coach I will help you improve whatever you want, including your income."

So I say, "Well, why don't you hire a coach?" and they say, "I can't afford one."

Well, wait a minute. If your whole pitch is that coaching improves someone, improves anything they focus on, including income, then why is it that if you want more income *you* don't get a coach?

They don't always see the contradiction in that, but I'll tell you what it is. The contradiction is that they really don't see how powerful coaching is because they are not experiencing it themselves. And if you don't have your own coach coaching you, in some way your income is going to fall way short of what it could be.

Also, it is very persuasive when you go to a prospect and you say, "Coaching has changed my life and it continues to do so today. I have a coach myself, and I believe in it because it works." Your prospect is more likely to listen to and hire you than if you say, "You know what? I don't have one. I can't afford coaching myself...ah....I don't quite believe in it, but I'm trying to sell it to you."

It would be like a doctor saying, "I don't go to doctors myself. I don't trust them... I think they do more harm than good, so I myself don't go to a doctor. I use natural healing. But please tell me what's wrong. I'll write you a prescription."

You wouldn't like hearing that from your doctor. So prospects don't like hearing from a coach that they themselves don't have one. It makes them very nervous. It makes them want to go home and think about it. Or there are the codes that prospects use, like "I need to talk to my wife." That's code for "No thank you."

Discipline #15: Leave the conversation in the context of possibility, not the context of affordability.

Most coaches allow a prospective client to hang up the phone in a context of affordability. In other words, the prospect leaves his talk with you wondering if he can afford you (no matter what you charge). He goes to his wife or business partner and says, "Hey, can we afford to lose this amount of money on coaching?" Of course they are likely to say *no* in this context of affordability, because you left him wondering whether he can afford you or how he will get the money.

That context of affordability is not a service to the prospect (or to me; nor is it likely to bring me a client).

So I don't want to let that happen.

Before our conversation ends I want to return the client and myself to the context of possibility. Even if we have slipped into the context of affordability, I want to re-direct the conversation to the context of possibility before it ends:

What's possible if we worked together?

Why would it be worth it to you if we worked together?

How would it be worth it to you?

What in your world that you would like to be different might be different if we worked together?

What's possible for us?

What would you like to change?

What do you want?

Why don't you have it now?

Tell me what you want and then tell me why it is not in your life right now.

If you can tell me why it's not in your life right now, you and I might be able to create a plan to work together to make that possible for you. What would that be worth to you? Would those results be worth that investment? You tell me. I'm not going to tell you.

Now we are back in the context of possibility.

Discipline #16: Limitation creates value.

When something is limited, its value goes up.

I read a story about a stamp collector. There were only two of a certain kind of stamp remaining in the whole world, so naturally they were very valuable. He owned one of them and when he finally got hold of the second one he *burned* it. The price of the first one went way, way, way up when he burned that second one. Way higher than the two of them combined. Because now it was the only one in the whole world. Limitation creates value.

So when someone knows that you are limited (which you always are as a coach, because you only have so many hours every week to offer to the world), they know you don't have that much availability. The fact that you *do* have an opening and are willing to consider them for it raises the value of your offer—always. Limitation creates value.

In our prosperity workshops we really go in-depth on how to express and make use of this discipline. I want limitation to be very present in my communication about what I have to offer someone, even while I am offering it.

Discipline #17: Be constantly aware of the danger of role reversal.

Don't allow the roles to become reversed in a conversation with a prospect. In other words, don't let them become the coach and you the client.

Don't become needy and put yourself in the position of saying, "Well, you know, anything you want, call me anytime, tell me when you are available..." as you fall all over yourself to talk to them. It's called *role reversal* when you do this.

Please keep in mind that *you* are the coach. You are the one considering adding someone to your list of clients. You *choose* clients based on their coachability—it's not the other way around. I have coaches come into my school who have it totally the other way around until they learn this powerful discipline. Their whole approach is *unlimited* availability—"I'll coach anyone with money. If you have money, I'll coach you. I don't care if you're coachable, I don't care who you are, I don't care if we succeed together. It doesn't matter to me—all I want from you is a check, and then we'll book time and get through it."

You can see that this approach is not strong. It does not get you clients. It has to be the other way around. Even if you only have one client and you have room for nine more on your calendar, you must hold your role. You might want a ten-client practice but only have one client. You still don't want role reversal to occur when you are talking to a prospect. You still don't want to be needy and falling all over yourself and totally available to this person. You want to be the *coach* in the conversation. Because if you will hold for that, if you will commit to that, you'll get clients.

If you can communicate from that LIMITED place in you, you'll get clients a hundred times faster (I was about to say "ten times faster," but I really do mean a hundred times faster).

Now, finally, **Discipline #18. Be great at what you do—not just good.**

It's really important that a coach be great at coaching. I know that sounds odd because you're thinking to yourself, "Well, how can *every* coach be great? That kind of diminishes the term."

Well, not every coach *is* great. You're going to have to understand that most coaches aren't. Most coaches just try to do coaching as a novel way to make a living.

I'm not saying every coach has to be great, but I am saying if you want to grow a really prosperous practice, aim for great and have it be something you wake up inside you every day. Have coaching be something you *consciously* and *deliberately* get better at every single day so you *know* you are moving toward greatness.

Become great through the books you read, the DVDs you watch, the people who coach you, the seminars you go to—this is to build *greatness* in you. This is not because there's something wrong with you and there's a missing piece—this ongoing learning builds you to be great at what you do. It's really important.

● ● ●

One final note. As you practice these disciplines, never forget that coaching really *is* good for people. Coaching is *so* good, *so* powerful. Coaching has to be good.

The thing that's so different between coaching and therapy is that you can be in therapy for five years and still not know exactly what's happened or gotten better; but coaching *has* to be good. People don't renew their coaching contracts if it's *not* working for them, if life is *not* getting better, if they're *not* transforming and hitting their goals. They don't just stay on with the coaching like they might with therapy. So there's a burden placed on coaching to really work, so coaches keep getting better and better at what they do. Coaches have to prove themselves with their work constantly or no one will refer people to them, clients won't renew with them, and they'll have to start their lives all over again. You have to be great at what you do for coaching to be your profession, and that's the good thing about it; that's why so many people have coaches now. *Because it does work.* Therapy is about the past—healing wounds. Coaching is about the future. It's about creating a future that's different from the future that would have arrived by default if you had no coach and no sense of creativity and no commitment.

That's why in practicing these disciplines you will change the future—for yourself and your clients.

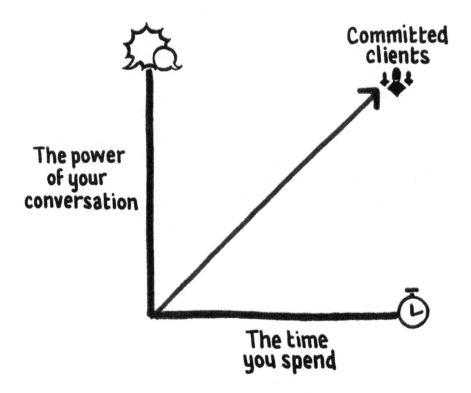

CHAPTER 15

Things you should simply **stop** doing

by Rich

THERE IS NEVER A REASON to make a cold call. Stop making them.

Stop wasting time on that website and that business card.

Stop hiding behind lengthy emails to potential clients.

Stop your need to create a huge email list.

Stop your thirty-minute taster sessions.

Stop trying to "market" what you do.

Stop going to networking events.

Stop trying to "get the word out."

If you are desperately trying to stay ahead of the internet marketing curve you are playing the wrong game. The internet is moving so fast you couldn't outrun it if you tried.

No high-performing client was ever created outside of a conversation. And no high-paying client was ever created outside of a *powerful* conversation.

CREATING CLIENTS

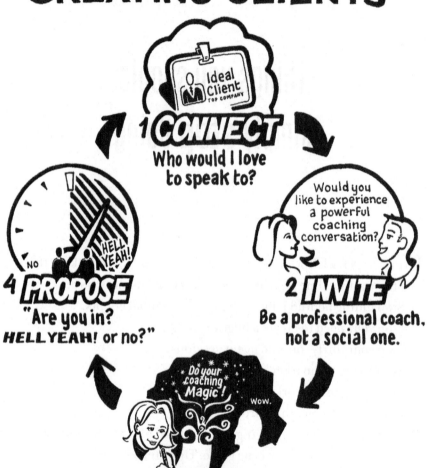

CHAPTER 16

Try this step-by-step process

by Rich

THERE REALLY ARE PROVEN steps to take for creating clients.

And they don't involve marketing or growing an email list or adding another thousand followers on Twitter. They don't even require social media, a website or a business card. Despite what the "experts" tell you.

This process is powerful. And it works. Take a look:

Connect → Invite → Create → Propose = CLIENTS

CHAPTER 17

Step 1: Connect

by Rich

THAT'S IT. ONLY CONNECT.

Ask yourself, who would I **LOVE** to speak to? And then call them. Bring your humor and curiosity. Be genuinely interested in what they are up to.

"Hey Sarah. Long time no speak. How's things? How's the family? How's the business? What are you up to? What's your next big project? What's your biggest challenge right now?"

At some point, when you are genuinely interested, you may see a way that you can support or be of service to her. There will be a book you can recommend. Or an article you can send her. Or a client you can refer to her. Sometimes you'll notice that the person you're speaking to is facing a challenge. Maybe they're struggling to turn a dream into a clear vision. Maybe they just inspire you.

That's when you go to the next step...

CHAPTER 18

Step 2: Invite

by Rich

THERE ARE TWO LOVELY QUESTIONS that change everything for a coach who is creating clients. "Would you like some help with that?" And "Who do you know?"

If you are talking to someone who you believe could really get value from spending time with you, there's a simple question to ask them when you hear them describe their dream, their challenge, or their biggest fear: *Would you like some help with that?*

If the answer is a clear *yes,* do **not** jump into coaching them in that very moment. Be like a doctor. If you meet a doctor at a party and you start to tell them about the problem with your knee, they won't ask you to roll up your trouser leg! They'll tell you to book an appointment.

So be a professional coach. Not a social one. If the answer to your question, "Would you like some help with that?" is a clear *yes,* invite them to meet with you. In person is always best, but over the phone can work perfectly. Block out two hours for them. Let them know that you will create a life-changing coaching experience. Don't be afraid to tell them that. Coaching IS life-changing. Even a single session.

Then put a date in your calendar.

The alternative, if you are speaking to someone you either imagine may be open to coaching or may know someone who wants coaching is to ask the question, "Who do you know?" It is so gentle and creates so much space that the person you are speaking to can relax and really hear your question without any of the natural resistance that most coaches create when they are trying to "get" a client.

"Christina, can you help me? I have a space available on The Confident Woman's Salon. It's a program for nine amazing women. Each woman is powerful, confident and successful. She has already achieved a great deal in life. And despite a track record of success, she is ready for support to achieve a goal that feels 'impossible' right now. Do you know a woman like that?"

Every once in a while, the person in front of you will say, "Oh my gosh. That's me!" But even if what you are creating is not for them, they won't feel you're trying to force something on them.

And if this isn't right for the person you are speaking to, they will pause and genuinely reflect on who they know.

Then, when someone says a name to you, never say, "Thanks, I'll call them." In fact, do the opposite. Get curious...

"Tell me about her. What's her big dream? What do you think may be holding her back the most in life, right now? Has she ever experienced coaching before? Do you think she'd be open to coaching? Why do you think she'd benefit from speaking to me?"

At the end of this conversation, if it feels like there may be a fit, say something like:

"Have your friend call me or email me. You see, I never cold call. Even for a referral. Tell her that this is my gift to her from you. Tell her that I'll block out two hours for her. I'll create a powerful coaching experience and we'll get her challenges handled. Forever."

Make your invitations as if you are inviting people to the best party in the world. Coaching is such a *gift* to most people's lives. Don't hesitate to share it. Because they'd be crazy to miss it. But even if they're not ready for it in this moment, that's perfectly fine, because someone else will be.

And when they are—that's when you get to create your magic...

3 CREATE

Serve them so powerfully they never forget your conversation for the rest of their life.

CHAPTER 19

Step 3: Create

by Rich

Most coaches launch into a bunch of logistics when you ask them about coaching. "Well, I speak to my clients once every two weeks for an hour." Or, "We meet face-to-face once a month." Or, "I'll send you my free ebook." Or, "I'll subscribe you to my video series." Or, "You'll have access to my member site..."

The problem is: no one cares!

Truly. Clients don't care about what you have to offer. They don't even care what you charge. They are too busy thinking about their problems or their dreams. Indeed, they only ever care about the answer to *one* question: *can you help me?*

The truth is they don't care if you're a coach, a consultant or if you can sprinkle fairy dust on them. *If* you can help them get what they really, really, really, *really* want, then they *will* find a way to become your client. So the real magic is not in your diplomas or coaching certifications. (Most of the very best coaches I know have *no* certification. Some have failed marriages, some went broke and some were fired from jobs. That's all irrelevant.)

Don't wait for one-hundred percent readiness. It will never come. When you are eighty percent ready, go for it. Run straight at it. Get exposed. Risk messing up.

The real magic is not in your self-belief or whether or not you think you can deliver a certain amount of value. The real magic is in whether you are willing to help your clients dive deeper than they have ever gone into the question: What do you really, really, really, *really* want?

Show up. Be present. Be bold. Coach them powerfully. Be relentless. Be Sherlock Holmes and explore deeper into their lives than anyone has ever gone with them.

Find a way to *create* an experience of your Coaching Magic for everyone you spend time with. Because then they will do whatever it takes to experience more of it.

CHAPTER 20

Step 4: Propose

by Rich

How much money did you make in proposals in the past thirty days?

A proposal is where you explicitly say to a person, "It will cost $X to work with me for Y months." It's a proposal when you find out what would be an inspiring vision for a potential client. It's a proposal when you tell them, "It's either a *Hell Yeah!* for both of us or it's a clear *No*." It's a proposal when you say, "This is how you make your payment. We begin the moment you send the money."

Most coaches have no idea how to make a proposal. A potential client asks, "What would it look like to work with you?" And the coach dives into logistics and hours and packages and options. Or they say, "Let me put something in writing and I'll get back to you…"

Don't be afraid of the money. It's just a number. Some people will say *yes*. Many will say *no*. And either is fine because you can move forward once you have a clear *yes* or *no*. Most coaches are so afraid of a *no* that they won't ever make a proposal.

"Rich, I loved this coaching session we just did together. How much do you charge?"

"Well, let's slow things down for a moment. Let's find out if it would really be a great fit for us to coach together. I have five criteria that any client must meet. My clients must be inspiring, or have an inspiring mission. They must make, or be ready to make, a big impact in the world. They must be fun. They must bring along a challenge; I'm not looking for an easy ride. And they must understand the power of commitment."

I'll pause to check in with the person in front of me. If they meet these criteria, I'll let them know. And then I'll go on.

"Would you like to hear a little more about how we could work together?"

You see, I'm continually seeking permission to continue when it comes to a proposal.

Then, based on our conversation, I will map out how our coaching will support their dreams, visions and goals becoming a reality. I will add to our conversation stories of results my clients have achieved or outrageous goals my clients have taken on. I'll share stories about my own goals and even my own struggles. I don't want to hide anything from my clients.

And only then, if all of this is still a fit, will I talk "logistics."

"This is how often we will speak or meet. This is how much support you can count on from me. This is how much your investment will be. And this is how you make your payment. This is what you can count on me for. And this is what I require of you, if we are to work together."

I will be very clear with them:

"Does this feel like we are rushing things? If it does, let's slow things down. Because if this doesn't feel like a fit, let's call it a clear no for now.

"Let me be clear: you do not need coaching. In fact nobody needs coaching. The question is, do you want coaching? Personally, I believe in coaching so much that I have had my own coach for years. But that's because I

"*Maybe...*"
"*I'll get back to you...*"
There's no such thing as "Hell Maybe"

love having someone who believes in me. I love having someone hold me accountable to a bigger vision. I love someone who doesn't believe in the negative stories I tell myself or the fears that hold me back. Not everyone wants that.

"Basically unless this is an absolute yes for you, let's leave today being totally clear that it is a no. That way if the desire begins to build in you to be coached you can come back to me. But only when you are ready.

"And if you decide you'd like to begin, the moment you make your payment you are in. Here's where you send your check..."

CHAPTER 21

Never take less than two hours

by Rich

A COACH I KNOW WAS shocked when I told him that I never spend less than two hours with a potential client. You see, he only ever spends twenty to thirty minutes in conversation with potential clients.

Dee Hock was the CEO of VISA, the first-ever trillion dollar company. He once said, "As a leader, I'll never schedule a meeting for less than two hours. Anything less than that and the issue should be dealt with by someone else."

I took that idea into my coaching. And I'll never meet a potential client for less than two hours.

CHAPTER 22

Don't close a sale—open a relationship

by Rich

It's interesting, and relevant to coaching success, how a woman once described the difference between meeting Gladstone and Disraeli in the week that they were both standing for election as the British Prime Minister.

She said, "After dinner with Gladstone, I thought he was the most interesting person in the world... But after dinner with Disraeli, I thought *I* was the most interesting person in the world..."

Disraeli won the election.

As a coach, be more like Disraeli.

Approach a conversation with a potential client from a place of being really, really present. Put all your attention on them and get curious. Ask questions about their life and their world. Ask about their dreams and desires, their fears and their pain.

And then, if—I stress *if*—you see a place where you could help, ask, "Would you like some support with that?"

I always come from a place of building relationships. I'm never trying to "sell" anything to anyone. Let me tell you a story about this.

While living in Beijing for a few months, I had a great conversation with a wonderful businesswoman. She was a successful entrepreneur, coach and consultant. And she inspired me with the reputation she had created for herself in working both with ex-pat spouses and also in the corporate world.

She asked for some support and I created a coaching session for her. We did some deep coaching but at the end of the session it didn't feel like she needed ongoing coaching. So, as much as I would have loved to have worked with her, I chose not to even suggest that we coach together.

Now at that point if I had only been interested in closing a sale, I'd have crossed her off my address book and gone out looking for other people to coach.

Instead, I opened a relationship. Over the months ahead, I emailed to check in with her. I sent her an interesting article. And at Christmas when she asked for a little support, I told her to call me and I coached her.

In the eighteen months since I'd met her, we'd stayed connected but she'd never paid me a thing or become a client. Then one day, she came to my mind and I had an idea. I emailed and said, "I've been thinking of you and I have something that I think may be a great fit for you. Would you like to hear a little bit about it?"

She said yes and called me. I explored her dreams with her for two hours. And at the end we discussed coaching together.

Then she sent me a check—a year and a half after we first met.

Imagine if I'd tried to close a sale at the beginning and then walked away when that didn't happen. Coaches do that all the time. They fail to see that this is a relationship business.

CHAPTER 23

Learn to astonish your clients

by Rich

W HEN WAS THE LAST TIME you *astonished* a client?

It's easy to lose sight of the fact that one of the most powerful ways to create new clients is to serve your current clients so powerfully that they never stop talking about you.

How could you astonish one of your clients today?

It usually doesn't take much.

Call a client the day after a coaching call for a five minute catch-up. Clients love to hear from you when it's not expected. Send a book to a client without telling them in advance. Offer to double the length of a coaching call, to really go deep with a client. Invite a client to a day-long, face-to-face session with you, instead of your usual one hour over the phone. Write a client a personal, hand-written note, right now.

Failing is not a problem
you will face.

Failing is how you
get there.

CHAPTER 24

Learn to enjoy enrolling

by Steve

To BE GREAT AT SOMETHING, anything, you must eventually enjoy the process from top to bottom.

If you never enjoy it, you are never going to be great at it. Even if you have a good month here and there, it will never feel natural, and you will slide back into despair sooner or later.

We are always good at what we enjoy, and we always enjoy what we're good at.

Then what comes first, enjoying it or being good at it?

It happens together. As skill improves so does enjoyment, and as enjoyment increases so does skill. Joy and strength arise simultaneously for the person who stays in action long enough.

CHAPTER 25

Sell the experience, not the concept

by Steve

What do I want my intake conversation, my long "getting-to-know-you" conversation with a coaching prospect to *demonstrate*?

I want it to demonstrate my curiosity, my love of coaching, my ability to relate a story or case history or two about people I've helped through coaching, my ability to listen, to relate, to get to the bottom of things, and my desire to convert dreams into projects so that my prospective client will stop *wanting* things and start engaging in the process of creating them.

Therefore I really want to take my time when I first talk to a client. And if my prospect has a website, blog posts or a physical place of business, I want to do good homework prior to talking to this prospect. That demonstrates commitment.

I always want to be the person who demonstrates what other people merely promise.

I have had many clients who could not "afford" me who ended up working with me because they sold something, or found a sponsor or benefactor, or got a loan, etc., so I learned never to factor in my own estimation of their ability to pay. I leave that up to them. People become really resourceful when they desire something. People usually get what they desire strongly in life. And I can only cause them to desire my coaching by making an amazing demonstration of what it can do for them.

CHAPTER 26

Actively seek exciting clients

by Steve

ALWAYS KEEP YOUR EYE OUT for great clients—high-functioning people who want to go from good to great. Coaching comes from the world of sports and the arts, where athletes and actors receive coaching so that their work will become *extraordinary* instead of just okay. Coaching gives clients a secret weapon, a competitive *edge* that their un-coached peers do not enjoy. Coaching takes people from good to great. Coaching is not for dysfunctional people. It is not there to heal the sick and wounded. It's there to help people reach their higher callings and *unlived lives,* the lives they are not living because they are trapped in their own isolated, self-critical egos. Coaching expands their world.

I could go on for a thousand pages about why coaching works and what it does and why it's great and how *unlike* anything else (including therapy) it really is.

When I have a friend who is willing to *refer* a client to me I will insist that *he* (my friend) take a two-hour session from me first so he knows what he is talking about when he refers me. We will never sell coaching by selling the concept or the abstract idea of coaching. We must *demonstrate* it.

I know I repeat myself, and I know it's fearless and good to do so.

CHAPTER 27

Possibility will trump affordability

by Steve

ONE OF THE PRIMARY AND most oft-repeated mistakes coaches make happens when they allow the end of a long intake conversation to focus on fee. On price. On affordability. On cash flow. On money. On scarcity.

So the prospective client hangs up and then walks away *inside the context of affordability*. And that's the worst place to end a call.

It's the last context I would ever deliberately create, and yet I've created it! It would be like if I were single and dating and just had a wonderful flirtatious and connecting, meaningful conversation with someone I want to see again, and I end the call with, "By the way, I own a meth lab. You need to see it sometime."

Please don't let *anyone* hang up or walk out the door if the last words you exchanged were about money. It's okay to go directly *into* the money issue, but then allow that issue to take you *back* to what your prospect *wants* and what his or her *opportunities* really are. You always want to leave your prospect inside the highest context of *possibility*.

Because about eighty percent of coaches end *every* call on the subject of money. Is that a total buzz-kill or what?

You've probably noticed that this is one of the Eighteen Disciplines—to always end the conversation on the highest *possibility* for the client, with the client doing the describing of that possibility. It bears repeating that when these disciplines are *practiced*, coaches become prosperous.

The coaches who are failing have no system for success. It's all about their mood and feelings. They take their emotional temperature throughout the day to determine what they will or will not do. If you see yourself in this sad portrait, throw your thermometer away and turn pro.

CHAPTER 28

Always be creating clients

by Rich

Good counselors lack no clients.

—William Shakespeare

NEW COACHES OFTEN HAVE no idea of the boom-bust cycle that most coaches face.

They work hard to enroll their first few clients and then, with a sense of pride, they dive into their coaching together. After a few months, these clients gradually complete their coaching agreements and suddenly the coach (who had been thoroughly enjoying their life and business only a few weeks before) discovers that they are now back to having no clients. And no income. And they have to begin the cycle all over again.

This is tiring. It is draining and dispiriting.

So what if you were *always* creating clients?

A new coach recently took a trans-Atlantic plane ride from London to Los Angeles. He told me that he chatted with the guy next to him on the plane. This man turned out to be an actor and he ended up coaching him during the flight. He also coached one of the airline stewardesses.

When he arrived in LA and an immigration official discovered his job, he even coached the officer for a few minutes. He was very excited as he told me all of these stories.

And then I asked him, "Did you tell any of them to call you when they get home? Did you get an email address? Or a cell phone number?"

He looked sheepish because the thought had never crossed his mind.

Clients of mine have created their own clients in the line at the supermarket and sunbathing on the beach. Friends of mine have created clients on airplanes, in trains and in taxis. You see, potential clients are all around you. The only thing they need is an experience of you and an invitation.

I met a woman in an airport and we began to talk. She asked what I do and I explained that I am a coach. We had a great chat and we swapped emails. A week later she sent me a message saying she had looked at my site and loved what I am up to. She said, "Let's meet up for a chat over coffee." I replied, "I don't really do chats. But if you would like to experience a deep coaching conversation, then call me. I will block out two hours for you for a powerful, life-changing experience..."

"Always be creating clients" is not about hard work. And if it feels like work then it's time to change the way you approach it.

It's more about a perspective on life. It's a reminder that all around you are people you can serve. There are people all around you who would love your support. Your only job is to ask if you can help.

CHAPTER 29

Be okay to begin as a beginner

by Rich

In the beginner's mind there are many possibilities.
In the expert's mind there are few.

—Shunryu Suzuki

WE ARE ALL FAMILIAR WITH the grading system in martial arts where you receive belts for different levels of mastery. Master coach Brian Whetten helped me see that building a coaching practice has a similar system of levels of progression.

1. At the **STUDENT** level you are a training to be a coach.

2. At the **BEGINNER** level you are a coach who regularly experiences the impact of coaching on your clients. (You have coached at least fifty clients.)

3. At the **NOVICE** level you are a coach who is regularly paid for coaching. (You have had at least ten paid individual clients.)

4. At the **COMPETENT** level you are a coach who can cover your monthly expenses with your coaching income.

5. At the **PROFICIENT** level you are a coach who can create clients by invitation or referral only.

6. At the **VIRTUOSO** level you are a coach who can create clients whenever you choose to.

7. At the **MASTERY** level you are a coach who can take extended vacations and/or create income while you sleep.

Notice that there is no timeline. This list isn't designed to restrict your success or slow your progress as a coach. However, it is designed to *inform* your progress, because just like in martial arts you have to master the skills at each level before you can move to the next.

It is helpful as a coach to see these levels of progression because it actually gives you permission to slow down and take time to really master where you are. When you know what game you are playing, this model also allows you to play full out—at the level you're at.

Use the "Litvin List" in Appendix 2 to determine your current level.

And remember: whichever level you're at right now, we've all been there.

FEARLESS
COACHING

CHAPTER 30

Magical vs magic

by Rich

Magic is just someone spending more time on something
than anyone else might reasonably expect.

— Teller (of Penn & Teller)

THE MAGIC OF FEARLESS coaching isn't in you, the coach. It's over there in the person being coached.

The magic of fearless coaching isn't about a style or a system. The magic is not in any one technique. You see, fearless coaching is not magic. But it *is* magical in its impact. Results will show you that.

Here are the key components of fearless coaching. Learn these, practice these, and your clients will thank you. And remember this: do not wait. Use them in your very first conversation with a potential client. Don't save them until after someone has hired you.

They are most valuable to you when a potential client experiences their power right away, right there in that very first, long and extraordinary intake conversation.

The 18 Key Components of Fearless Coaching

1. Be bold.

2. Search for the Glimpse of Genius.

3. Go deeper.

4. Be okay with silence.

5. Keep some of your attention on the inside.

6. Remember that the magic is in the person in front of you.

7. Pay attention to their words.

8. Lead powerfully.

9. Hide nothing.

10. God with a small "g".

11. Come from Spirit.

12. Set a clear intention.

13. Seek permission.

14. Coaching creates miracles.

15. Invest in yourself.

16. Be YOU.

17. COMMIT.

18. Be willing to fail.

1. Be bold.

Say boldly what needs to be said. And hide nothing. You are not there to be their friend. You are there to create the most powerful coaching they have ever experienced.

As a coach, your only mission is to wake up each morning and ask yourself: "Who can I serve so powerfully that they never forget our conversation for the rest of their life?" When you serve people in this way you will become an *extraordinary* coach.

2. Search for the Glimpse of Genius in the person in front of you.

My clients tell me that one of the biggest gifts for them is that they know I always believe in them, even when they forget to believe in themselves.

The high bar you set for your clients has nothing to do with how much money they make, their job title, or the size of the company they work for. It has everything to do with *your* criteria for dream clients. My own clients are inspiring, and they make a big impact - or they are ready to. They are committed. They are fun. They bring a challenge to the table. And I ruthlessly seek out these criteria in any potential client I spend time with.

3. Go deeper.

Be on a relentless quest to go deeper than they ever imagined they wanted to go. Find their "secret dream"—the goal *behind* their goal.

You can only create extraordinary clients when you are willing to ask them questions that no other coach would ask. Dig deeper into their deepest dreams and their secret fears than anyone else has ever gone.

Every client has a goal behind their goal.

And no client ever comes to you for the first reason they present to you.

Your job is to find out what they really, really want. Do that and they will thank you forever. And you will have all the clients you ever want.

4. Be okay with silence.

Learn the power of the pause. It is one of the most powerful coaching tools.

Do not coach until you have a client in the room. Wait until you are certain what they really want. And know that if you are speaking more than they are, you are unlikely to uncover what is really going on inside them. If you don't have a question to ask, say nothing.

Fearless Coaching in Action #1

A client who is a coach sent me a worried message. He was concerned that a potential client might not want to hire him as a coach after their first conversation.

I told him: Your worries are irrelevant to your conversation with him. Instead, put your attention on this man. Fully. And serve him so powerfully that he never forgets your conversation for the rest of his life. When you are done, ask about his relationship and his business and the amount of money he is making and his dating life and the *legacy* he wants to leave in the world... And then offer to help him with these things. *Serve this man so powerfully that he never forgets this conversation for the rest of his life.*

He may become a client right away. And he may not. But he might make a referral. Or he might come back to you in a year. Or two. Or three. There's a longer-term game here too.

5. Keep some of your attention on the inside.

What you are feeling on the inside is an incredible coaching tool. We are all deeply connected. So, keep a small percentage of your attention on the inside of your body. Slow down. Because what they are feeling, *you are too*.

Don't be afraid to use your intuition. Don't be afraid to say what feels uncomfortable. Don't be afraid to let the person in front of you acknowledge feeling uncomfortable.

6. Remember that the magic is in the person in front of you.

If you give them your absolute, full, undivided attention and you get really present, your inner wisdom will tell you where to go next.

Listening is the most underrated skill for a coach. You do not need to be an expert in your client's life or business. They didn't hire you to be a consultant. They hired a coach. I have coached CEOs, soldiers, Hollywood executives and Olympic athletes and I didn't have to know anything about what they did in order to help them create remarkable results.

In fact, as a coach, one of your gifts is that you know less about their business than they do. So don't be afraid to say nothing, or even to ask questions that seem obvious.

7. Pay absolute attention to the words of your client.

Because their language creates how they see their world. And how they see their world *becomes* their world. If you are prepared to listen deeply, their words will tell you everything that is going on in their world.

As a coach, when you meet a client whose behavior does not make sense on a surface level, you can know for certain that deep down there is a level at which the behavior makes perfect sense.

The results your clients are generating perfectly correlate with the actions they are taking. But if you can't help them find out *why* they are taking those actions, the actions will never change.

Pay rapt attention to their words. Because their words tell you where they are focusing. Change their focus and you change their world.

8. Lead powerfully.

Refuse to buy into any story your clients may bring with them. Challenge how they see the world. They do not need sympathy. They do not need you to be their friend. *"But this is who I am..."* is not an absolute. It is a *choice*.

Coaching requires passion and authority. Never forget who's the coach and who's the client.

9. Hide nothing.

Show up fully expressed; show the real you. Hide nothing; hold nothing back.

Fearless Coaching in Action #2

A client showed up full of doubt and concerns about her choice to move halfway around the world and begin a career as a super-yacht broker (selling multi-million-dollar ocean-going yachts). Our coaching session anchored into her psyche just how powerful she is, and within days of her arrival in a new country she had created connections with captains of super-yachts, successful boat dealers and owners of super-yacht boatyards.

In our next session she questioned whether I tell all my clients that they are powerful. "I do!" I replied. But purely because I **only** work with powerful clients. I set a very high bar for who I will work with. And I reminded her that she was one of these clients.

10. God with a small "g".

Notice just how powerful the person in front of you is. Put your attention on their power. One advantage of me spending so much of my own life feeling powerless is that I now quickly see how powerful people are. But this is something we can all do.

Your client is the god of their world because they *create* their own world. And they don't even know it.

11. Come from Spirit.

This isn't about you. Tap into something deeper. Your purpose. A higher calling. The universe. God.

You cannot be a powerful coach if you think this is all about you.

12. Set a clear intention.

Get clear on where you are speaking *from* and where you are speaking *to*.

Speaking from your head to their head is only one way to coach. Try speaking from your heart to their inner wisdom. Or from your gut intuition to their heart.

13. Seek permission.

The more safety you create, the deeper you can go. "Would it be okay with you if I ask a question about that?"

14. Get clear that coaching creates miracles.

And let your client know that. Set a powerful context for every coaching session. Increased expectations will call out the best in both of you.

15. Invest in yourself.

Because you can't take a client any deeper than you have gone yourself. I have invested hundreds of hours and over a quarter of a million dollars to receive very deep coaching from some of the world's most impactful

Fearless Coaching in Action #3

I once sat down with a young woman who was a millionaire. In her early twenties she sold her first company for over a million dollars. Now in her mid-twenties, she shared her goal to make seven-figures a year in online income.

Smiling, I said that I wasn't interested in coaching her around this goal. She seemed stunned and said, "But every coach I meet says they'd love to coach me!" "Of course they do," I replied. "With your track record there's no doubt that you'll achieve that goal. But I only like to coach people around goals that make them feel truly alive."

So I asked her, once you've got your $100K a month, what else do you want? And then we went deeper. What else? What else? What else? (I am like a dog with a bone with this simple question—and I won't let go until I see the sparkle in their eyes.)

We talked for about an hour until she was overcome by emotion. With tears streaming down her face, she told me about the incredible challenges she'd had to overcome. And finally she admitted that she really wanted to inspire young entrepreneurs to live healthy, balanced lives in order to make a bigger impact. "Now we're talking!" I said.

coaches. I *believe* in the life-changing power of coaching because I have *experienced* life-changing, powerful coaching.

16. Be YOU.

Because there is no coach like you in the world. And that is priceless.

17. COMMIT.

Play FULL Out.

18. Be willing to fail.

Again. And again. And again. As Sir Winston Churchill once said, "Success is stumbling from failure to failure with no loss of enthusiasm."

Barbara Kingsolver wrote: "The very least you can do in your life is to figure out what you hope for; and then live inside that hope." As coaches we can do better than that. Life really can be amazing. So why not have your clients find out what they really, really want—and then help them to create it. Hope is irrelevant. Coaching makes miracles occur.

John F. Kennedy once said: "The only reason to give a speech is to change the world." It's actually the only reason to have a powerful conversation with *anyone*. Fearless coaching means *every time you coach, you change the world*.

Fearless Coaching in Action #4

I coached a well-known actor, who came to me one day very upset that her project had been given to an A-list Hollywood star, just as production was about to start.

You might think her anger and frustration were reasonable—she certainly thought so—and when I refused to buy into her story she was stunned. Instead, I explained that she had created a **Perfect System** for the results she was getting.

I took a risk and allowed this coaching session to explore deeply into her experiences, fears and beliefs. During the coaching she shared with me some traumatic situations she'd faced as a child. And as I went deeper still, we uncovered two deeply held—yet contradictory—beliefs. The first was, "I will be safe once I am successful." And the second was, "If I really have success, people will take advantage of me."

This first belief had led her to greater and greater success and even fame because much of her motivation came from the idea that the more successful she became, the less people could take advantage of her.

But the other belief of her **Perfect System** resulted—again and again—in opportunities being "taken away" from her at the very last minute. You see, if she achieved too much success she could really be taken advantage of and there was no way she would let that occur.

I suggested that when the studio executives told her, "Sorry, we're giving this project to someone else," she had just crumbled and accepted it because she was secretly relieved

She didn't seem to believe me.

Then I asked her what would have happened if she had looked them in the eyes and said, "I don't give a **** how famous the other actor is. She's not me. No one has been through the experiences that I have. No one understands this project like I do. There is no one in the entire world who could play this role with the passion and tenacity and courage that I will bring to it."

She looked at me, blinking slowly, and said, "Oh my God."

And she just paused, in silence, for several minutes.

Finally she responded, "I really could have said that to them..."

It doesn't matter who your client is, they are paying you to be one of the few people in the world who is willing to say the things that no one else will say.

CHAPTER 31

Coach and coach and coach

by Steve

I have no special talent. I am only passionately curious.

—Albert Einstein

YOUR ACTIVITIES ARE GOOD, but through all this good preparation and contact-making don't forget to coach. Get a client NOW and start coaching, whatever you have to do to do that. Remember that you build a coaching practice by coaching people. No other way to do it. No reason to delay.

Get with people and coach them. Have long, long, involved phone conversations. No one will want coaching because of an email or anything like it. Just as a brain surgeon would not send emails promoting brain surgery.

Enjoy the fact that you are a coach now!

Take some interested person who has "no funds" and coach him for two hours. He'll *find* the funds for more work with you.

Many of my most lucrative coaching contracts came from people who had no resources. Or so they thought. Until their lives were so profoundly changed by a long coaching session that they went to their

Aunt Millie and borrowed money from her to *continue* working with me. Aunt Millie saw it as an investment in her nephew's education. It worked for everyone.

Coaching leads to more coaching.

CHAPTER 32

Learn to love those feisty **no's**

by Steve

Don't worry when someone says no.

You will be surprised at who comes back to you later with a fee in hand after originally backing away at the thought of paying such an amount.

Sometimes weeks, sometimes months and sometimes years later, but proposals generate future business. We just don't see it because our culture's attraction to the negative has us translate a proposal that gets a *no* into "emotional disappointment."

A *no* can be the best and most exciting thing about a coaching practice, but only after we practice a lot. And learn to really *feel* how fun they are. How powerful.

Yes lives in the land of *no*. Without *no* there could be no *yes*. *No* means you are in *action*. Only passivity can stop you from being prosperous.

If someone in another city, unseen by you, flipped a coin a lot of times, could you tell me how many heads they got? No, you couldn't even make a good guess unless you knew more information, right? Okay, well, what if I told you how many tails they got? Would you then be in a better

Yes lives in the land of no

position to guess how many heads? Absolutely! Why? Tails and heads go together! You get them both when you flip.

Yes and *no* go together, too. So if I know how many *no's* you got last year, I'm in a much better position to tell you how many clients you have.

CHAPTER 33

Truth is what clients value

by Steve

Let your prospects know what coaching with you would be like by having your intake conversations be long, extremely real and truthful. You are selling coaching, so don't mince words or do the dance of money-fear by flattering them, chatting them up or acting in ways that disgust your own heart and soul.

Instead, be willing to listen deeply and then be the *first* person in their lives to tell them the truth. Be real and tell the truth about how you *really* see their problems.

Remember, too, it's not just a numbers game.

It's not just the luck of the draw. "Talk to enough people and sooner or later one will cave in."

It's not that.

Just find *one* person and coach that person. Then move on. That's really how coaching practices are built.

Don't focus on massive numbers, because that takes your attention away from quality of listening, quality of conversation. It's all about the *next* person you talk to, not the number of people you talk to.

Slow down and focus. Stay on the path.

CHAPTER 34

No such thing as plural

by Rich

YOU ONLY EVER HAVE one client to worry about.

This client.

The one in front of you *right now*.

One of the *biggest* mistakes coaches make is to think in terms of *plural*.

Singular is all there is.

The client in front of you *right now*.

Really deeply see, in the most relaxed way possible, that there is only one person to converse with and enroll into your coaching. Choose that person slowly and wisely, and focus your life on her life.

Then create a safe space and be the first and *only* person in years to deeply desire that she shares everything with you.

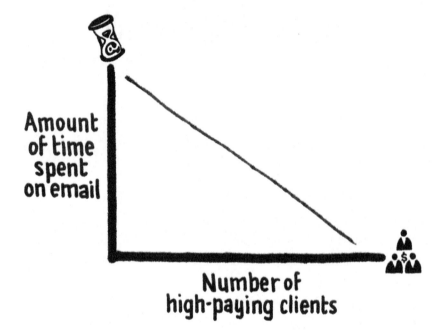

CHAPTER 35

Sometimes the best email is no email

by Rich

YOU WILL INCREASE YOUR BUSINESS tenfold if you respond to almost every prospect's long email with the words, "Call me."

Too many coaches get stuck behind their computers, crafting lengthy emails. As a coach, your power is in a conversation. Get into a conversation. As soon as possible.

"Call me!"

CHAPTER 36

When you **do** use email, do **this**

by Steve

WHEN YOU DO SEND EMAILS, make certain they always contain value for the recipient and are not just requests that benefit you.

And when you check back with someone who is out there "considering" working with you, make sure your communication always offers a fresh new idea and added value, and is not just an attempt to *check in.*

In other words, because we are coaches gifted at creating transformation and delivering the tools of personal growth, we should make sure we never miss that opportunity!

We should never turn into someone who is just selling.

Although where possible we always want to upgrade our communication with a prospect from email to phone, from phone to in-person, from in-person to climbing a mountain together, etc., there are times when an email *can* be powerful. So don't be afraid to have your email be strong and clear. Here's one I once sent to a prospect, and it *got me a coaching client.*

Dear Bill,

You said you want to hold off on the conversation with me until you know what my "templates and approach" are.

There is no approach, and no standard coaching template. You yourself are the agenda and you are the approach.

We work on the lies, the self-deception and the fears in you about money, and about the power you perceive to be outside yourself in other people. We work on your difficulties with "making decisions" and inability thus far to make bold choices in life and follow through and trust yourself completely to do so.

I have no coaching approach. Transformation is the only objective. And the irony for some people is that the very thing that they want the coaching for (an indecisive, half-hearted life) is what's keeping them from deciding whether to get coaching.

When you're ready you'll call me...meanwhile I am attaching an ebook I wrote called Powerful Graceful Success because I know it will help you to the next level.

Steve

Focus on the person in front of you. Ask yourself, "How can I serve this person so powerfully that they never forget this experience for the rest of their life?"

CHAPTER 37

Push past the fear and get closer

by Steve

SELLING IS HARD WHEN we fear other people.

Coaching must become fearless to succeed in big ways. Coaching is all about courage and creativity. You can't skip that.

If you *feel distant* from your prospect, you won't sign them as a client. When you fear them, you cannot be direct. You have to think of how to best hint at your intentions or throw shallow, needy, pitiable *info* at them.

Coaching is not about "information." It is about transformation. Change someone's life and they will hire you. All other activities are weak-kneed and wimpy and will have you quit this profession in absolute despair.

Client enrollment becomes more fun and effective the *closer* we get to the other person.

One way to get closer is to put yourself in their place and give them the level of truth *you* would want.

Another way to get closer is to *ask them* all the things you wonder about them. Such as why they have not yet achieved what they say they want to achieve.

CHAPTER 38

Strength comes from getting uncomfortable

by Rich

Do one thing every day that scares you.

—Eleanor Roosevelt

A POTENTIAL CLIENT ONCE ASKED me, "Rich, is there a way to coach me so I can pay your fee with no hesitation?"

I replied, "I *want* you to have hesitation before you begin coaching with me. This isn't supposed to be an easy decision. This is supposed to be one of the biggest commitments you've ever made. This is supposed to have you lean right into your edge. You do not *need* my coaching. And if you want to coach with me, you will find a way for that to happen."

In my experience, the more my clients commit, the more they achieve—because they are fully engaged. So if you wish to create a coaching practice with high-end, high-performing clients, you have to be willing to *challenge* them to make a big commitment in order to sign up with you.

Get comfortable feeling uncomfortable and your world will change.

CHAPTER 39

The biggest mistake coaches make

by Steve

THE MISTAKE IS THIS: They don't honor the person they are selling to. They place their own needs and fears ahead of the prospect's.

They don't enter the prospect's life and solve a real problem. They stay inside their own offer and their own worthiness. They do this subconsciously, but they do it, and it pushes the prospect away. It makes the prospect defensive. Soon the prospect doesn't even want to return a call.

If we can learn to love being in the prospect's world and solving the prospect's problems and bringing out the best in our prospect throughout the session, we will always look forward to this process we used to call "enrolling" or "selling"—because now we just call it "fearless coaching."

CHAPTER 40

Stop being a pro bono bonehead

by Steve

Too many coaches tell me that they spend a lot of their time helping their "friends" with their problems. They smile and say that's why they became coaches, because they're so good at that.

But why are you happy helping people who are not paying you?

I would look at that.

Because you *could* be helping people who are paying you. And when you do that, both parties benefit MORE than when you give away all this free help.

Free advice is usually taken with a grain of salt. But a paid session can change someone's life forever.

There is a profound difference in the listening a paid customer brings to a professional session compared to the listening they bring to "a chat with a really nice person I know."

You help the world *more* if you do your altruistic work *after* your coaching practice and income are over the moon. That's the time to start giving yourself away pro bono, when you choose to. For now, remember to put the oxygen mask on yourself first, before trying to fit it over the mouths of others.

If you were working for an employer in a nine-to-five job, the employer would not give you time off real work for you to "help others." You'd have to do that after your professional work was complete.

One of the biggest problems coaches have is not bringing the same professional work ethic to their coaching practices that they would to a "real" job. Once a coach wakes up to that, she is back on track toward prosperity.

CHAPTER 41

Extraordinary results are created by extraordinary requests

by Rich

THINK OF A CLIENT. Or a potential client.

Or a colleague. Or a friend.

Or someone you don't yet know.

Now make an Extraordinary Request of them.

And then another.

And then another.

It will change everything.

One of my clients was an ex-military man. A soldier who was personal friends with CEOs, royalty and millionaires from all over the globe. He realized that many of the wealthiest and most successful men on the planet were simply bored. They were tolerating life. They had no real challenges remaining for them because they had all the money they'd ever need. However, there was still something missing.

So my client designed an extremely high-end program that would give men like this an opportunity to really face their edge. You see, these men were craving adventure. And my client's military and personal-protection training made him fascinating to these people.

I helped him craft the enrollment for the program. There would be no website. For men like this it needed to be so exclusive that it had to be word-of-mouth only. And we were clear that the initial coaching conversation had to give them a full-on *experience* of what this program would offer.

He began to reach out to the men he knew. One person at a time. And then, each time he saw a place where he could support them in their life or on their mission, he made an extraordinary request. He asked one man to climb a mountain with him while he coached him. He invited another to swim across a freezing lake and another to join him on a helicopter flight. From that moment on, he had such fun inviting people to speak to him, that it was inevitable the people he reached out to would want to know more. And when they did, he made the boldest requests of his life.

Despite his military background and having spent a great deal of time in combat situations that would terrify most of us, his biggest fear was of having a sales conversation. It was initially very intimidating to have to share details of a program that included a fee of $150,000, paid in full and up-front. But even that fear began to transform over time as he made one extraordinary request after another.

CHAPTER 42

Don't charge for what you do

by Steve

You aren't billing for time elapsed. You are billing for the very real possibility of a goal being achieved that would not have been achieved without fearless coaching.

Your client has a default future that will occur on its own if his life does not change.

When he pays you he is paying for his life to change.

He is paying for his dream to be converted into a project. You will be the project manager. (In businesses, good project managers make six figures.)

If all you talk about is "per hour" and how long the sessions will go it demeans the real value of coaching. Your client has hired you because of something *they* want to do differently. They know deep down that it's true what Walt Disney said: "If you can dream it, you can do it." That's what they will pay for.

Also remember you are charging your client for the breakthrough they wish to achieve instead of the "things they get," like sessions, emails, spot coaching, in-person meetings, and so on. You can say

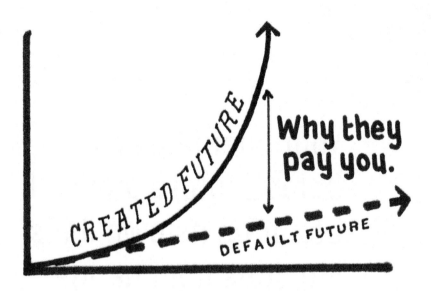

that "at a minimum" you'll get these, but you want to have your intake conversation establish the *goal*.

Maybe your prospect wants out of her career rut. What would that look like? Let her describe the rut to you. Have her really take her time to describe it, and all the feelings it creates in her. This is her default future. *Now* let's talk about what's possible. Help her see what might be possible through the work you might do together. And that possibility, that goal, that breakthrough *is* the product she is paying for. Would she pay you money to get out of that rut and learn to *fly again*, and to know how to always get out of ruts in the future? Of course she would.

Your client has a default future that will occur on its own if his life does not change. When he pays you he is paying for his life to change.

CHAPTER 43

The best time to plant a tree

by Rich

COACHES OFTEN SAY TO ME, "I wish I could create such deep, impactful coaching conversations." Or, "I wish I knew how to charge high fees for my coaching." When I hear this I smile, because there was a time when I couldn't do these things. There was a time when I was terrified to say my fees out loud. There was a time when I felt too intimidated to challenge the beliefs of the person sitting opposite me. There was a time when I barely believed I could be paid money for coaching. And it wasn't so long ago.

I had spent my entire working life with organizations, and once a month money was simply transferred electronically to my account by my employer. Only a few years back no one had ever looked me in the eyes and handed me a check for my services. And I had never *imagined* that someone could smile and say thank you as they gave me their money.

When I lost my job in the British education system I used my final paycheck to spend six months living on a beach in Southeast Asia. It was there that I began to use the coaching skills I'd learned in my previous leadership roles to coach and support my fellow travelers.

I remember the very strange moment when someone first asked, "Can I pay you for this?" And I remember the even stranger moment when I first said "Yes..." and they handed me some cash.

The first amount of money I was ever paid for coaching was 200 Thai Baht (that's less than five dollars). Fast forward a few months and I had signed up my first-ever monthly coaching client for ten dollars per month.

But I promised myself that I was never going back to work in an organization. I was never again going to have a boss. I was committed to being a coach. It didn't matter what I was paid, I was going to astound people with the possibilities they couldn't yet see for themselves.

I remember an early dream to have five personal coaching clients a year at $25,000 a client. I practiced saying this number out loud. I'd say it to the mirror. I'd say it to my wife. I'd say it to my friends. And with some trepidation, I began saying it to potential clients.

At first, nobody entertained this number. And I had to get creative. I helped someone write a blog to help pay my bills. And I designed smaller, three-month and six-month coaching programs. I even had a man from Greece pay me for a single hour of coaching that we split into four fifteen-minute sessions over two months.

And then, almost eleven months since I had begun saying out loud that I charge $25,000 for a year of Deep Transformative Coaching, a woman looked me in the eyes and asked, rather matter-of-fact, "How do I pay you?" She sent a check that day, enclosed in a lovely thank you card.

Fast forward a few years and clients now pay up to $75,000 to work with me one-on-one.

You see, my coaching is *bespoke*. This is a British word that historically referred to a man's suit that was tailored *precisely* to the buyer's specifications. My coaching is highly personalized and tailor-made. It's the reason my clients pay in full and in advance for their coaching.

How I got here isn't magic.

But it seems it isn't for everyone.

The latest research states that eighty percent of coaches make $20,000 a year or less. And the majority of them are working part-time.

One of my Apprentices signed his first-ever $50,000 client within the first month of us working together. He billed $400,000 in coaching fees, with a few high-end clients, in our time together. He signed his first three $50,000 clients and then his first $100,000 client—and he still doesn't have a website or a business card. The year before he hired me as a coach he billed $15,000.

And what was even more powerful than this were the results his clients began to generate in the world. In fact, one of his clients just met his goal to raise twenty million dollars for the first phase of his dream project. Suddenly his coaching fees don't seem so large.

There is such power in this work we call coaching. And our clients get that. I have noticed that the thank-you notes I receive have gotten larger as my clients have written larger checks. Your clients are paying you to help them achieve their dreams. So help them dream big and stay with them along the course. Raising your fees is not hard when you can see the incredible results your clients are creating.

The best time in life to plant a tree was twenty years ago. The second best time in life to plant a tree is today.

Don't wait. Coach people.

Don't wait. Raise your fees.

Don't wait. Make bold proposals.

Don't wait.

CHAPTER 44

Don't be a wallflower: Tell your story

by Steve

"I DON'T USUALLY TALK ABOUT my accomplishments."

That's what a coach (now a good one!) told me a couple years ago when he was just learning to get clients.

I was not easy on him when he told me that.

In fact I said to him, "Bingo! Check your bank account. Go online right now and look at it. Or call your bank and ask what the balance is. Because you can trace the amount of money to the words you just said: *'I don't usually talk about my accomplishments.'*"

If I am your prospective client and I'm thinking about working with you, I *want* you to be proud of your accomplishments, and I want you to be easily conversant about them.

Because it gives *me* confidence in my decision to work with you.

It makes my decision so much easier. Not only that, it makes our work together more effective if as the client I'm not wondering if this humble guy, this "nice person" coaching me has any power, skills or moxie at all.

I will question your value when you are self-effacing and shuffle around the floor with your head hung low in a hang-dog, "little ol' me" countenance.

I want a coach who knows who they are. Who knows how good they are, who knows their accomplishments and who isn't at all shy or uncomfortable talking about them.

If you can't freely discuss your accomplishments in a relaxed and enthusiastic manner, how can you possibly be the coach who can change my life?

Finally, by not talking about your accomplishments in colorful ways you are not being fair to me, your prospect.

You aren't giving me enough to go on. So I probably won't decide to work with you. And therefore, in the name of maintaining a certain safe, shy and humble "personality," you are denying people a chance at transforming themselves and solving their problems.

So step up and be bold. For their sake and yours.

Drop all that fear-based, fake humility and stop trying to win friends and influence people. Instead, step up and change a life.

CHAPTER 45

Stop schmoozing

by Steve

schmoozing: *present participle of schmooze. (verb)*

1. Talk intimately and cozily; gossip.

2. Talk in such a way to (someone), typically in order to

manipulate, flatter or impress them.

The Oxford Dictionary

SCHMOOZING, CHATS, LONG LUNCHES and social time confuse your client into thinking that coaching is a lot of friendly chatting together... And why do they want to pay for that?

Take the three hours you will *lose* traveling to lunch, having lunch and traveling back from lunch and put them into a *powerful* intake session.

And notice this email, just received from a coach who gets it:

I signed another new client. She came to me as a referral from a friend that I spent four hours with coaching for free. I really slowed down with my friend, gave her the best I have and asked for nothing in return. I only served.

Then two days later she referred me to her friend. I slowed down and connected deeply and powerfully. In the past I would not have given myself the permission to take that much time with a person I did not consider a prospect on a work day.

Thanks for the speaking the truth.

The truth I spoke was a recommendation that this coach convert his focus from pleasing people (and winning them over) to fearlessly serving them right out of the box.

It's time to lead

by Rich

Gentle in what you do. Firm in how you do it.

—**Buck Brannaman**, *The Horse Whisperer*

JAMES WAS A POTENTIAL CLIENT. He asked to have a session with me. And then he cancelled. By text message. I was willing to reschedule and suggested two alternatives. But then I received his email:

Mondays and Fridays are very tight. Mondays I'm only free between 10:05am and 1:15pm and Fridays I'm only good between 9:30am and 1:00pm. Try again.

This was not the sign of someone who was committed to a coaching experience with me. It was time to do what I call *firing a potential client*. I have a rule of thumb for life: *Hell Yeah! or No*. And potential clients who are not yet a *Hell Yeah!* for a conversation with me are not where I choose to invest my energy.

Sometimes it's just great to help those people become either a firm *yes* or a firm *no*.

So I resisted the urge to send a long email and wrote:

Call me. I need 5 minutes of your time. That's all it will take.

When he called, I explained that for the moment we should take this session off the table. Maybe coaching wasn't a priority for him right now. And that was fine. I just wanted us both to be clear.

Well, sometimes people surprise me. He replied, "Oh no. I really value the time with you. I don't want to give the impression that I am not interested. How about if I send you my calendar, so *you* can pick the time for our call?"

Ten minutes after our conversation, I received this message:

Rich—Next week I am free on Tuesday all day and into the evening. Wednesday I'm free until 2:00. The following week I am again free Tuesday and into the evening. Wednesday I'm free until 4:00. Thursday I'm free until 2:00. Friday I'm free between 9:30 and 12:00. The week after that I'm free the same times on M, T, W and Th.

Your clients want you to lead because it gives them permission to be leaders in their own lives. Do not be afraid of stepping into your power as a coach.

DEEP INNER
WORK

CHAPTER 47

Coaching is NOT a luxury

by Rich

COACHING IS INCREASINGLY recognized as an essential part of professional and personal development.

Eric Schmidt, the CEO of Google, said, "Everyone needs a coach." The Harvard Business Review reports that coaching is a one-billion-dollar-a-year industry.

A Manchester Consulting Group study of Fortune 100 executives reported that "coaching resulted in a Return On Investment of almost six times the program cost as well as improvements in relationships, teamwork, job satisfaction and quality." And a recent survey by The Hay Group International stated that "between 25 and 40 percent of Fortune 500 companies use executive coaches."

In the past coaching was seen as a luxury. But as we have faced a global economic downturn over the past few years, coaching is increasingly accepted as a necessity in order to develop your career, to get to the next level in your organization, to make more money or even to build better relationships.

So the challenge facing most coaches is not that there are too many coaches or that people do not want coaching. It's that most coaches—even coaches at the very top of their game—do not know how to create high-paying, high-performing and highly committed clients.

Once you embrace that challenge and drop all the unwarranted pessimism around imaginary "competition" and "low demand," your career will take off.

CHAPTER 48

The secret: there is no secret

by Rich

A COUPLE OF YEARS AGO I was invited to speak at an event for a hundred coaches and consultants who wanted to get more clients. I was one of the last speakers, on the third day.

Over the first two days we listened to a range of presenters who each told us they had the key to success. There was a woman who told us that the way to grow a successful coaching business was by speaking from the stage. And boy was she good at what she did—there were people streaming out of the room to buy her products before she'd even finished speaking!

Then there was a speaker who told us that success would follow when we wrote a book—and by the way, she had a secret system to teach us how to write a book in a weekend! Yet another speaker told us that using Facebook and Twitter was the key to success. And so they went on, each with their own special, unique way to be successful.

And it was strange. As each one spoke, I began to believe them…

Maybe *I* should be growing my business by speaking from the stage, or by writing a book, or by using Facebook and Twitter.

And then I caught myself.

I was doing what I often used to do in life.

I was looking for a guru, or a teacher or an expert.

Someone who would show me the Secret to Success.

A quick secret key that would help me jump over all the other steps.

But this time I caught myself.

You see, I have discovered what works.

For *me*.

And so, finally, I got up on stage.

But I didn't share a secret, and I didn't offer a system. I didn't create any scarcity about what I had to offer. I just talked passionately about how I built a successful coaching practice with a small number of high-paying clients with no networking events, no internet marketing, no email list, no business cards.

As well as my successes, I shared my fears and my struggles along my journey too. I told the story of how I began coaching on a beach and that my first ever client paid me $10, and that I made $4,500 in my first year of coaching. And I told the story of the marketing coach I fired when the only impact of using internet marketing was to slow down my business.

I shared some of the most powerful things I have learned about the game of creating high-paying clients.

And people seemed fascinated. They asked tons of questions. And—with no products or even a workshop to sell—I was surprised to have a line of people wanting to talk to me at the end.

I was really moved by one woman who came up to me in tears. She said, "Thank you for letting me know I can find out what works for *me* and go do that. Thank you for showing me what is possible."

And that was it. I knew I had to share what I had learned.

But there is no secret.

I know coaches who write a weekly newsletter and coaches who use internet marketing. My own coach charges $150,000 a year. You pay in advance and fly to Arizona for your face-to-face coaching sessions.

But I also know a successful coach who will only coach over the phone in fifteen-minute sessions. And one of the most successful women coaches I know runs workshops with three other female colleagues for powerful and unique four-on-one coaching sessions.

One of my friends has been a coach for over fifteen years and he will still only coach you for a maximum of three months because he puts such a high value on freedom. If you want to sign a six-month agreement, he says (with a smile): "No. I don't know what I'll want to be doing in three months' time. But if in three months you would still like coaching and I would still like to be coaching, then we'll talk."

Me, I rarely coach for anything less than thirteen months because I love to watch my client's total transformation over the course of a year together.

What I love about coaching is that *you* get to make up how you show up.

Try stuff out.

Find out what you love.

Be creative.

Be *you*.

There is no secret.

CHAPTER 49

The value of daily practice

by Steve

Rᴵᴄʜ ɢᴀᴠᴇ ʏᴏᴜ ᴛʜᴇ ᴇɪɢʜᴛᴇᴇɴ magical elements of a fearless coaching session (Chapter 30). I have never seen anything like that taught anywhere by anyone in the world of coaching.

Practice those components and you will become transformative.

But do practice them.

I gave you the Eighteen Fearless Disciplines that are proven to work in the art of client acquisition (Chapters 13 and 14). If you practice them.

If you are a coach, your work is good work, and badly needed by the client you don't have yet.

Imagine that client going through life without support, without a structure for raising self-awareness, without someone to tell the truth to, without a prosperity guide or a spirit guide. Imagine that person not having any of those things because you decided not to practice today.

All this coaching success stuff is *practice, practice, practice.*

Practice, practice, practice.

It only looks like magic.

Your clients want you to lead because it gives them permission to be leaders in their own lives. Do not be afraid of stepping into your power as a coach.

CHAPTER 50

If you want to do this, NOW is the time

by Rich

I<small>T IS TIME TO LET GO</small> of your fear of being bothersome, pushy or disliked.

It is time to be completely authentic so that people can trust you.

It is time to start asking for what you really, really want.

It is time to only coach clients whom you absolutely love.

It is time to master the way you communicate.

It is time to make bolder proposals.

It is time to get comfortable feeling uncomfortable.

Raising your fees is
not hard when you
can see the incredible
results your clients
are creating.

CHAPTER 51

Stay focused on what helps people

by Steve

STAY FOCUSED ON THE help that your making money will be for others.

Choosing to make good money and choosing to really make a difference in people's lives will be the same thing. They go together. You can't pull them apart.

So just keep focusing on those good actions you're taking, and on the proposals and invitations you're making, and figure out ways to sit down and *be with* people, so they can experience *you*—not just the idea of you.

Become more than a concept.

Start enrolling and coaching folks now.

And please know that this in turn benefits others, your clients, much more than it benefits you, because had you not enrolled them they would have spent that money on something that does *not* grow and transform them, often something misguided and foolhardy. They (looking at the statistics) would not have saved that money.

So when they hire you they have now truly invested in the one and only surefire investment there is: their own growth as an effective human.

CHAPTER 52

Service: energy out = energy back

by Rich

THE UNIVERSE RELIES ON a simple principle: energy out equals energy back.

Creating clients works this way too. When you put your energy into total service, the energy flows back to you in the form of clients and wealth.

But—and this is important—you can never have an expectation that if you really serve someone they will become your client. That's called being needy. You want instant gratification from the outside world instead of long-term strength-building inside you.

However, if you wake up every morning and answer the question, "Who can I serve?" you can then offer your attention and your energy to the first person who comes to mind. Now you connect with them. And you serve them. In the very best way you can.

- You email them an article.

- You call to check in with them.

- You offer them a coaching review session as an ex-client.

- You look at their website and send them a book that will support their mission.

Then let go of any needy attachment to them becoming a client, or even replying to your email or returning your call.

If you serve someone new every day, your world will transform as a coach.

CHAPTER 53

Never propose marriage ten days after you meet

by Rich

THAT WOULD BE MY ADVICE to anyone who asked. Nope. Never, ever propose to a woman ten days after meeting her.

Except I did.

I met my wife at a workshop in San Francisco. And I knew I wanted to marry her nine days later.

I guess I like to take my time with life-changing decisions. So I waited a day!

Then I asked. And she said yes. And as I write, we've been together for six years.

Most of the time it's never right to make a proposal to a coaching client very soon after meeting them. Building a powerful relationship is key. Often the vey best thing when you are enrolling clients is to *slow down* and really build strong relationships. Over significant time.

And yet every once in a while you just know...

Every once in a while, I'll meet someone and I'll just know: *I'd love to coach you.*

These days I'll simply tell them that.

Steve and I have a friend who is a coach who fills his practice every year by writing a few handwritten letters to the five to ten people he would absolutely *love* to coach that year. Each letter is so personalized with so much attention on that individual that they cannot help but be moved by this man.

So: who would you *love* to coach?

CHAPTER 54

Who are you being?

by Rich

W HO YOU ARE BEING SPEAKS far louder than how you describe what
you do as a coach.

I recently walked past this sign store in Los Angeles and snapped a
photo as I laughed out loud! The store has had a broken sign above its
own shop for months now.

How would your coaching practice change if you were never again
allowed to "tell" people what you do? What if, from now on, the *only* way
for people to understand what you do is for them to *experience* the power
of your coaching?

Most coaches end every conversation on the subject of money. Instead, always leave your conversations on the highest context of possibility.

CHAPTER 55

They pay for more than the hour

by Steve

YOU MAY THINK YOU JUST got a client at a $400 per hour fee. But you did not.

Please keep in mind always that it's not really *per hour*. She is paying for *many* hours of coaching experience when she writes you a check. Sometimes many years. When someone babysits, they charge per hour because you are paying for the hour they spend watching your kid. That's it.

When people pay a coach like you they pay for everything you've ever done, because you'll be bringing all that to the table. Not to mention all the books you've read, seminars you've attended and the other work you do (including *being* coached in profound ways) to make yourself the best coach you can be. So she's paying for that, too.

A woman once saw Picasso doodle on a napkin in a restaurant and she went over to his table and asked him how much she'd have to pay to have that napkin. He said, "$20,000."

She said, "What?!? I watched you, and it only took you five minutes to do it!"

He replied, "No madam, it took me my whole life."

CHAPTER 56

Think exponential versus incremental

by Rich

Exponential growth looks like nothing is happening,

and then suddenly you get this explosion at the end.

—Ray Kurzweil

THE DICTIONARY EXPLAINS THAT something is said to increase exponentially if its rate of change is very rapid. Conversely, the definition of incremental is a slight, often barely perceptible increase.

The problem is that most coaches are playing an incremental game.

They raise their prices from $100 a session to $120 a session.

They spend hours designing websites that make them look like every other coach.

They are more concerned about the graphics on their business card than where their next client will be.

A few years ago I began my coaching career by setting a goal to offer a thousand free Instant Confidence sessions. I began to tell people what I was up to, and within three months I had run four hundred sessions with people from all over the world. Truth be told, I thought I had a clever way to get clients. I later discovered that things don't work that way. Free thirty-minute sessions were always unlikely to be a way for me to create year-long, paying clients.

However, something unexpected occurred: I coached four hundred people in less than ninety working days and, boy, did I build my skills *exponentially* as a coach.

A few years later I spent a day with a coach, sharing the principles in this book. He immediately began applying them. A week later he signed his first $50,000 client.

Nobody said that change has to be slow or even hard. To live an exponential life, you have to be willing to do things differently and be open to the possibility that *everything you want is closer than you think*.

CHAPTER 57

Time to stop being so busy

by Steve

WHEN I'M IN CLIENT-CREATION MODE I have to remember that busyness is laziness. It's lazy to be busy.

It's lazy for me to occupy myself with all these small tasks when I know deep down that none of them will produce wealth. This "busywork" is an enemy to my financial success.

But there's good news. Something I discovered really helped me with that. I began looking at my day, my list of things I wanted to do, and I asked myself *which of these tasks will create income and which will not?* I then put a *star* next to the things that would create income, and I gave those things my most focused, lavish, creative, committed and clever attention.

I mean, I really took my time with those. I slowed down and connected with the tasks and people that I starred on that list. It has never been a waste of time to do that.

Most busyness comes from our wild, ongoing attempts to please others. Notice I didn't say *serve* others—I said to please them and win their ongoing approval. That kind of shallow, egocentric "busywork" is an enemy to your financial success.

Pleasing others is the real reason why people don't succeed. And in the end pleasing others doesn't win any respect from them either. So you lose both games. Be bold and hold to your boundaries. Look at the activities and people you have placed a *star* next to and choose them. Nourish those relationships slowly and creatively.

CHAPTER 58

Slow down to speed up success

by Rich

A martial arts student went to his teacher and said earnestly, "I am devoted to studying your system. How long will it take me to master it?" The teacher's reply was casual, "Ten years."

Impatiently, the student answered, "But I want to master it faster than that. I will work very hard. I will practice every day, ten or more hours a day if I have to. How long will it take then?"

The teacher thought for a moment then said, "Twenty years."

WHEN I FIRST MET STEVE CHANDLER, he told me I reminded him of his puppy, which would run around the house really fast. When it got onto the tile floor in the kitchen, its little legs would still run at twenty miles an hour but it stayed in one place like a cartoon character!

I was trying to do *so* much...

But I had it wrong. You see, *space is where miracles occur.*

And so I began to create space for myself.

And I *slowed* everything down.

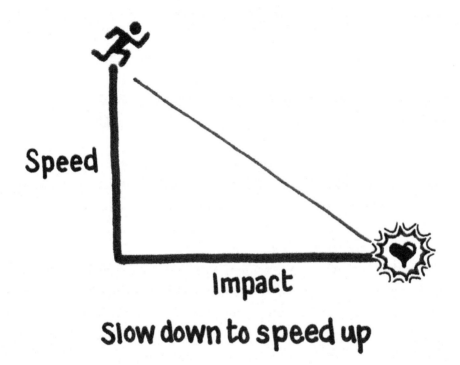

Slow down to speed up

Slow down your conversations with clients and you will notice things they can't yet see. Slow down your intake conversations with potential clients and you will create space for them to delve deeper into their lives than ever before.

Slow down the time you spend preparing for a meeting with a new client and you will think of questions that no one has *ever* asked them. Slow down enough to get a sense of your client's world before you meet them and you will be more present for them than anyone else has ever been for them.

Thomas Edison was a genius who invented the phonograph, the motion picture camera and the electric light bulb. But he was also a terrible fisherman. He used to spend an hour almost every day fishing but he never caught any fish.

If you are wondering why a genius would be obsessed with fishing when he was so bad at it, you are not the only one. Someone once asked him why he was such a poor fisherman. He replied, "I never caught any fish because I never used any bait."

When they asked why he'd fish without bait, he responded, "Because when you fish without bait, people don't bother you, and neither do the fish. It provides me my best time to think."

It was definitely no coincidence that the world's best scientist was also the world's worst fisherman. Edison really got the power of silence, the power of space and the power of slowing down. And one day, fishing with a bamboo pole, he had the insight to try bamboo as the filament for the first ever electric light bulb.

Practice regularly setting aside time for yourself to do *nothing*. Put time on your calendar for committed, quiet, creative time. And practice making this time as important a priority as a meeting with a client.

Even coaches who are already thriving and who want to get to the next level can benefit from slowing down their enrollment process.

CHAPTER 59

You can do this as a blue collar job

by Steve

Not long ago I got a message from a friend who is a coach in Greece.

She asked me what to do "when my energy gets low, and my hopes do too??!! That's how I feel today and although I know it will pass, a message about picking up the energy would be such a blessing!"

This was a wonderful question and I'm glad she asked it. In my non-prosperous years I would ask this question a lot. What do I do when I lose my hope and energy?

And then, in later years, because I had a rather wonderful coach, I was able to ask *him* the same question about what I should do when hope was gone. (Which is why coaching is so great—you get to ask and solve anything and everything.) He allowed me to see something.

If I have a game to play, my energy and hope are not problems. They are high. But if I have no game, no process goals, no scheduling of my own activities, then my moods plunge.

It's similar to this: I used to coach writers and authors when they were struggling with "writer's block" and not making progress on their books. Their hope and energy were low, so they did not write.

What I had them do was create a game, a scorecard, a schedule for logging the minutes or pages each day, with a *win* possible every day if they completed the assignments they gave themselves.

I would ask them, "Do you think truck drivers have this same problem? Is there something called Trucker's Block, where a driver wakes up and finds his mood isn't right for driving today?"

No. A trucker drives his truck no matter what his energy or hope levels are.

He has a schedule and a destination map, and he follows it no matter what.

So in coaching the trick for me was to find a way to make as many of my activities be *lunch pail, blue collar* activities as I could. So mood would not be a factor. Hope could come or go, it didn't matter. My energy would be high or low and I'd still do what I set myself up to do.

That takes practice. Logging a certain amount of conversation and invitation time each day. Making a certain amount of proposals each week. Measuring my activities, not my results. Staying in the game.

It's only when I think coaching success is different, fundamentally, than success at a blue collar job that I get confused and emotional about it.

It's no different. It obeys the same principles.

The other day I asked a coach if she had any clients the previous day and she said no. So I asked if she had put eight hours into securing new clients into her business.

She said, "You're kidding, right?"

Because to most new coaches that would be an absurd, ridiculous amount of time creating clients. Having conversations. Inviting and proposing. In one day? Eight hours?

Yet the person I saw today at the motor vehicle department goes to work and has conversations for eight hours every single day. What's the difference?

The motor vehicle department employee is committed to keeping her job. The coach is obviously not. The coach figures she'll try this for a few more months and if it doesn't work out, she'll just blame the profession itself.

Instead, engage people in conversations that serve them and you. You can't be in a bad mood while you are genuinely helping another human being. The mind can't do both things at once.

Put up an activity scoreboard. Make it a game. Declare destinations. Follow your maps. A trucker's life works for you, too.

Life can be a full of hope and energy for all of us blue collar coaches.

Free advice is usually taken with a grain of salt.

But a paid session can change someone's life forever.

CHAPTER 60

No one ever pays for coaching

by Rich

MOST COACHES APPROACH potential clients with the view:

THEY have ALL the money. But I'm just me...

Successful coaches know:

They ALL have money. And there is no one else in the world like ME!

You see, no one is ever really paying for coaching.

When I meet someone interested in coaching, I ask them to tell me about their dreams. And then I help them to dream bigger than they have ever dreamed before. Then I help them see a way they can really, truly create that dream in their life.

I once had a session with a sixty-five-year-old woman who was exploring coaching with me. At the end of our conversation she cried. She told me she was crying because she had never shared her dreams with a living soul, including her husband.

So the truth is your clients are not really paying for your coaching. Or even for your way of being. (Although both are important.)

Your clients are paying for their dreams. And their dreams are *priceless*.

If the person in front of you has a big enough dream and they get that spending time with you will help them to achieve it, they will hire you.

When you put a client in touch with their dreams, they still have choice. After all, no one *needs* a coach. But if they really get that spending time with you will help them, your clients will find a way to create that money.

A new coach recently asked me, "Is coaching just all about money?"

Here is something interesting I have noticed: the *only* coaches who ever ask me questions like that have no money.

No. Of course coaching is not all about the money. But the money you make is all about your coaching. Money is a *result* of your impact, your service and your creativity. Increase one or more of these factors and your life will transform. And so will the lives of your clients.

Money is a sign of the impact you are having in the world. More money in your bank account means you are making more of an impact. Bank account low? Find a way to make a bigger difference in your clients' lives.

Money equals service. If you want to make some money, wake up and ask yourself, "Who can I serve today?" And then create a way to serve them even more powerfully.

Money is the most perfect expression of your creativity. If your bank account is low, it's a reminder that it's time to get even more creative.

Remember, too, that money is only good for one thing: it's good for buying stuff. But most people want money for the feelings it will bring. So when money comes in, they feel good. And when it doesn't, they feel awful.

Break that cycle quickly as a coach.

Stop tracking and celebrating your billings. They are out of your control. Instead, celebrate the amount of money you make in *proposals.* Proposals are in your control. Billings are not. Increase your proposals and your billings will follow.

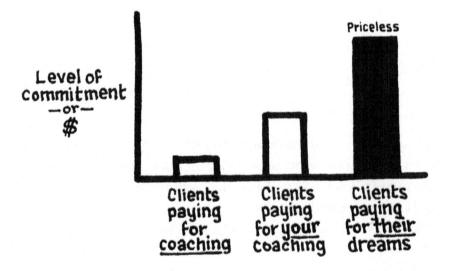

CHAPTER 61

Learn the beauty of a routine

by Steve

THE COACHES I COACH sometimes tell me that they have had a bad week or a bad month because they were "down" or discouraged or burned out.

They want to know how to change their attitude or mindset.

But attitude is not what's missing.

What's missing when bad weeks or months occur is a routine.

The beauty of a *routine*, a practice—*a committed amount of time I devote to something no matter what*—is that it does *not* rely on enthusiasm or "feeling like" doing it or the "spirit moving me."

The routine of building a coaching practice through conversations is simple and it works. The only problem people have is with stopping. They do it for a little while and then get distracted.

If you want your practice to grow, design a routine. Then follow it every day. Then change the routine next week, but put a new one in place.

Your alternative is to check in with your feelings all day long to find out what you're up for. This leads to financial disaster, in case you haven't noticed yet.

The coaches I know who are failing have no system set up for success. They pretend they don't know about routines or systems. It's all about their mood and feelings. That's what governs their actions. They have the professionalism of a toddler. They take their emotional temperature throughout the day to determine what they will or will not do. If you see yourself in this sad portrait, it may be time to throw your thermometer away and turn pro.

CHAPTER 62

Fail and fail and then fail more

by Rich

I've missed more than 9000 shots in my career. I've lost almost 300 games.
Twenty-six times, I've been trusted to take the game-winning
shot and missed. I've failed over and over and over again in my life.
And that is why I succeed.

—Michael Jordan

MY FRIEND CHRYS IS currently training for his third dan black belt in Kempo Ju-Jitsu, one of the toughest martial arts on the planet.

Many years ago, four friends (including Chrys) and I showed up for our first martial arts class. We all did well and we loved training and we took one grading after another. But gradually each of us hit a plateau. A moment where we couldn't seem to improve, no matter what we did.

And within five years, one after another, we quit.

Chrys didn't. He stayed in the game. He's been training in this martial art for over twenty years now and he's pretty incredible at what he does.

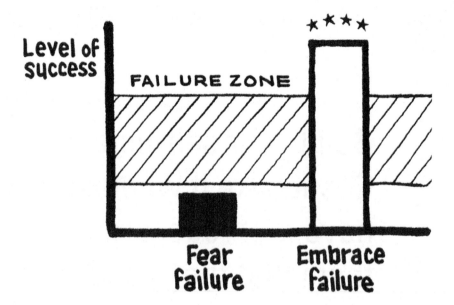

But twenty years ago Chrys was no better than any of us. Actually, he laughs that back then he cared less about the gradings than any of us (which is probably a big part of his secret).

If you want to be successful as a coach then get ready to stay in the game. There will be times when nothing seems to work. Stay in the game. There will be times when everyone is saying *no*. Stay in the game. There will be times when you seem to make mistake after mistake. Stay in the game.

I used to think the key to success was to do my best. But (as usual) I had things the wrong way round. Samuel Beckett got it right when he said:

Ever tried. Ever failed. No matter.

Try again. Fail again. Fail better.

Sometimes I will challenge my Apprentices—who are already thriving coaches—by saying that we will have no coaching session next week if they don't screw something up in the next seven days.

Safety is the enemy of success. Be proud of your mistakes. Take a risk. Fail spectacularly. And then go out and fail some more.

Build your self-esteem. Clients like it when you have it. It reassures them that they have picked the right person.

CHAPTER 63

Why would a coach need a coach?

by Rich

Invest in yourself, in your education. There's nothing better.

—Sylvia Porter

Any time I meet a coach who doesn't have a full practice I ask if they have ever invested money in their own coach. Many (too many) coaches have not.

No wonder they struggle to create a thriving practice—they don't believe in investing in their own coach but they want their potential clients to invest in one.

"Well, do you have a coach?" a potential client asked me, with a wry smile.

"Actually, I have three right now," I said.

"What!" she exclaimed. "You're a coach. What do you need three coaches for?"

"Oh," I said, "I don't need any of them. I want them…"

My clients get just how much I believe in the power of coaching when they hear that I've invested over $250,000 on my own coaching. And as I share my own successes, they are able to see the possibilities that coaching can create.

Find a coach that will be right for you. Don't hesitate to ask a potential coach for stories of the financial, emotional and skill-building impact of their work. Ask for a deep experience of how they coach.

(And as a cautionary note: research whether or not the coach actually does what they say they do. We have seen book-writing coaches who have never published a book, internet marketers who run coach trainings but don't have any clients and social media coaches who have thousands of followers but no income. But these are stories for another book.)

So, the truth is you don't need a coach.

In fact, nobody needs a coach.

Don't let anyone tell you otherwise.

But if you want to increase your own impact and income as a coach, you might want one.

CHAPTER 64

Learn to log in and log out

by Steve

No SALE EVER TOOK PLACE outside of a conversation.

I remember years ago when I had to log in and log out.

When I woke up I kept a captain's journal like in *Star Trek*, and when I spoke to someone I logged in. When I was finished, and now *outside* of the conversation, I logged *out*.

Like punching a time-clock. Blue collar. Because I knew that if I wanted to have my own business, every single moment I spent outside— logged out—of a conversation was a self-defeating waste of precious time and a deliberate self-destruction of my business. A lazy man's cry for help is to passively fail to do what he knows would get the job done.

And my "laziness" was only fear.

Boy, I remember those days so well. Then, each day's end I would report to my coach at the time, Lindsay Brady, exactly, down to the *minute*, how much time I'd spent logged in to my true work that day.

When I made those numbers, those minutes, increase, and then increase again, and then more and more, my business just totally took off.

Later I saw that minutes—actual minutes spent in conversation—were the final deciding factor, the final *cause* of my success. It was never some magic marketing bullet or appeal or anything else I'd been pining for.

It was a rough period for me. Some months my wife Kathy and I looked at less than two thousand dollars in income that month. Not ideal! But the turnaround came from logging in and not logging out.

Anyone can do this. Anyone willing to be fearless about logging your communication minutes each day.

CHAPTER 65

Grow your professional self-esteem

by Steve

WHEN YOU LOSE CONFIDENCE in the value of what you have to offer, it gets harder and harder to ask for a good fee.

Because people ultimately pay you not what *they* decide your coaching is worth, but what *you* decide your coaching is worth.

Exchanging money is always an exchange of energy. Sometimes it's just the energy of thought, but it's still energy.

And it's hard to bring that energy up from a place of low self-esteem. There isn't a lot of energy down there!

So one of the best ways to keep your confidence and your sense of value high is to save and read your fan mail.

Any time you get an email complimenting your work, save it. Save all of the rave reviews for anything you do in a certain file. Keep a little journal or notebook. If somebody calls and thanks you or compliments you, jot it down.

Because there's going to be a time next week or next month where, before you go into a very important call or meeting, you're going to want to read through those notes and really get *who you are.*

We let our self-esteem slip.

By not paying attention to the subject. But self-esteem is destiny in this business. You can have low self-esteem at the Department of Motor Vehicles and still be Employee of the Year. It won't work in this business of fearless coaching.

And sometimes it takes another person to come in and boost us and remind us how good we are. Sometimes our romantic partner plays that role and pumps us up before we have a big, important conversation. But don't rely on that. Better to be in charge of that function yourself. After all, it is called *self*-esteem.

And clients like it when you have it. It reassures them that they have picked the right person.

CHAPTER 66

Learn to suffer a little injury

by Steve

THE GREAT PHILOSOPHER Emerson said: "Our chief want in life is somebody who will make us do what we can."

Well, that's good news for coaches, because that's our job description. Amazing that our job description happens to match up with everyone's *chief want* in life.

So it helps to keep in mind that *everyone* wants what you've got.

Then why is it so hard to sell?

Answer: It's not.

It's just that for most of us (especially me) selling did not come naturally. It wasn't learned in childhood. It certainly wasn't learned in school (which usually teaches the complete opposite of free enterprise).

So we have to *learn it* as adults. And ninety percent of adults never learn it. It's a brand new learning.

And why is that such a challenge? Maybe Dr. Thomas Szasz says it best:

> *Every act of conscious learning requires the willingness to suffer an injury to one's self-esteem. That is why young children, before they are aware of their own self-importance, learn so easily; and why older persons, especially if vain or important, cannot learn at all.*

Rich and I wrote this book to deliver this learning. To produce a safe and fun place to learn this exciting, challenging skill of enrollment that some call sales. We are here for one purpose, and that's to teach it to you. You are not alone anymore. Highlight the parts of this book that scare you and wake you up. Go back and read them aloud every day. And put them into practice until you are independently wealthy.

CHAPTER 67

You are the one you are looking for

by Rich

Don't ask what the world needs. Ask what makes you
come alive, and go do that. Because what the world needs
is people who have come alive.

—Howard Thurman

I SPENT MOST OF MY LIFE searching for a secret principle—or even a special teacher or leader—that would show me the way. You see, I was convinced that there was a secret way to be successful and happy at whatever I was doing.

I did meet many extremely successful and happy, world-class coaches. I tried hard to be like them. But it never quite worked. The more I tried to be like other people, the less authentic I became.

And it's very hard to do what you love when you feel inauthentic. It's very hard for people to be drawn to you when you don't feel authentic yourself.

For most of my life, I thought that if I could be more like other people, well, *then* I would be successful. Then I would have a life that I loved.

What I slowly began to see as I got to know some of the world's very best coaches was that none of them were trying to be anyone else.

And as time went on, the more I risked being myself, the more wonderful my life became.

Who knew that I had it the wrong way round for so long?!

Be YOU.

There is no one like YOU in the world. In a planet of 6.5 billion people, YOU are a very, very scarce commodity.

The more YOU you become, the more you will draw the right people to you.

The more YOU you become, the more *fun* your life will be.

And the more YOU you become, the more your clients will pay.

As Dolly Parton said: "Figure out who you are and then do it on purpose."

CHAPTER 68

Five frogs are sitting on a log

by Rich & Steve

THERE'S AN OLD RIDDLE THAT says five frogs are sitting on a log. Four decide to jump off. How many are left?

What's your answer?

Take your time.

No rush.

Take a moment to consider your answer.

How many are left?

The answer is five.

Why? Because four "decided" to jump off. That's all they did. And there's a big difference between deciding and doing.

We did not write this book just so you could have more information. Who really needs more information? If you're a coach, and if you're ready to actually jump off the log, this can be a book of transformation for you.

Just decide what tiny action you will take today to create your next client.

And then take it.

Don't wait for one-hundred percent readiness. It will never come. When you are eighty percent ready, go for it. Run straight at it. Get exposed. Risk messing up.

Failing is not a problem you will face.

Failing is how you get there.

CHAPTER 69

The **end** is really the **beginning**

by Rich

EVERY TIME I WATCH A Hollywood romance with my wife, I am amused that the credits begin to roll just at the moment the guy gets the girl, or just as they say their wedding vows.

My wedding day was one of the happiest moments of my life. But it was really just the *beginning* of my relationship. Monique and I have had ups and downs. We've faced challenges and we've struggled. We have moments when we can read each other's minds and we feel totally in love. And we have moments when each of us wonders, "Why I am with *this* person who doesn't understand *anything* I say or do?" (Plus, "Why oh why won't he do the washing up like he promised?")The way you create a thriving relationship—one day at a time and one conversation at a time—is also the only way to create a thriving coaching practice.

The end of this book is just the beginning of the *next* stage of your coaching practice.

Let go of any need for a "magic" system for creating clients. Instead, focus on the person in front of you right now. Ask yourself, "How can I serve this person so powerfully that they never forget this experience for the rest of their life?"

And be prepared for a miracle to occur.

mir·a·cle [mir-uh-kuh l] *noun*

an effect or extraordinary event in the physical world

that surpasses all known human or natural powers

Dictionary.com

Here's an example of a recent miracle I got to watch close up—and a great reminder to me that thinking I know the "right" way to do something is *exactly* what stands in the way of having more of my own miracles.

My wife, Monique DeBose, is an incredible singer/songwriter who helps people use their "small" voice to express their "Big" voice in the world.

She had been hard on herself because all the time she had put into raising our son over the first year of his life meant she might never get her career back. She was concerned she'd no longer be able to make money doing what she loves.

A while back we visited London and Monique arranged one of her Creative Vocal Improv events. She didn't advertise it. She simply contacted a few people. And she only charged £10 per person.

Only two people signed up. And then one of them cancelled at the last minute.

Now the truth is, I myself engaged in a little bit of judgment: "Obviously" she should have advertised the event. "Obviously" she should have asked people to share it with their friends. "Obviously" she should have charged more...

Now, I have learned the first rule of relationships: never give my wife "advice." So I chose to keep quiet. But I was actually quietly judging from the sideline.

When I got home that night Monique was crying and I was really worried until she told me that the one person who did show up brought along two friends. They were all so impacted by her work that they were literally moved to tears. It turned out that they all work for an extremely well-known media company. And, they said to her, "You should come and train our company. We really need you."

One of those three women is in charge of training and they have invited her to train their company when we are back in London.

You know, life really can be exponential. You are *far* closer to everything you want than you could ever imagine. Miracles are far closer than you think. And there is no one "right" way to do anything in life. Woody Allen was correct when he said that eighty-percent of success is showing up.

Be YOU.

Because there is
no coach like you in
the world.

And you are
priceless.

creating an
EXTRAORDINARY
coaching practice

The Litvin Levels

What level is YOUR coaching practice?

THE LEVELS BELOW DON'T ACTUALLY exist; they are made up! But coaches find it powerful to discover where they are on their coaching journey. You *will* go through each of these levels to become a thriving coach *but* there is no prescription as to how long this will take. Each level could take years, weeks or days. This document was designed to inform and free you—not to limit you.

Following the table there is space for you to jot down any insights that come to mind and the action steps you can take to move to the next level.

My Coaching Practice Level:	**STUDENT COACH** I am studying or training to be a coach.
To reach this level:	**Master the Art of Practice:** Train with and learn from the very best.
How to move to the *next* level:	**Stop "helping":** Seek permission for every coaching conversation you have.
How to remain at this level:	I don't understand the distinctions between coaching, consulting and helping. I tell people what to do and try to solve their "problems."

My Coaching Practice Level:	**BEGINNER COACH** I have experienced the impact of coaching clients. I have coached at least 50 clients.
To reach this level:	**Master the Art of Invitations:** Learn to enjoy inviting people to a coaching conversation.
How to move to the *next* level:	**Coach your butt off:** Your only job is to fill your calendar with coaching conversations. It does not matter whether you charge for them or not.
How to remain at this level:	I coach too few people. I only coach my friends/family. I coach without permission. I compare myself to more experienced coaches and feel overwhelmed by what I believe I need to do, so I do nothing.

My Coaching Practice Level:	**NOVICE COACH** I have my first 10 paid individual clients.
To reach this level:	**Master the Art of Coaching:** Coach, coach, coach, coach!
How to move to the *next* level:	**Sell the experience:** Find ways to create powerful coaching experiences for people *before* you discuss coaching them.
How to remain at this level:	I put my attention on "getting" clients instead of creating ways for people to *experience* my coaching. I spend too much time on "getting the word out" (growing an email list, making a beautiful website, designing business cards or on Facebook/Twitter). I'm afraid to ask for money for coaching or I set my fees so high that no one pays me. I am pleasing my clients instead of powerfully and vulnerably serving them.

My Coaching Practice Level:	**COMPETENT COACH** I can cover my monthly expenses with my coaching income.
To reach this level:	**Master the Art of Powerful Proposals:** Be willing to feel uncomfortable. Serve, don't please.
How to move to the *next* level:	**Get a coach:** If you don't believe in coaching enough to hire your own coach, why would your clients do the same with you?
How to remain at this level:	I still charge an hourly rate for coaching. I believe that people can't afford coaching. I haven't created a list of powerful "hero stories" of things my clients have accomplished. I don't believe enough in coaching to invest in my own coach. If I've paid for coaching, I've never paid more than I feel comfortable spending (although I hope my clients are willing to do just that). My life still contains people, places and things that *drain* me of energy.

My Coaching Practice Level:	**PROFICIENT COACH** I can create clients by invitation or referral only.
To reach this level:	**Master the Art of Deep Coaching:** Serve them so powerfully they never forget your conversation for the rest of their life.
How to move to the *next* level:	**Find their "secret dream":** Go deeper than any other coach would dare to go. Be bold. Get your client in touch with their "secret dreams," because their dreams are priceless.
How to remain at this level:	I coach people too soon, before I have discovered what they really, really want. I coach people around the *actions* holding them back instead of helping them go deep enough to become aware of *how they see the world*. I don't spend time creating a lifestyle I love. I don't invest in training or coaching to support me creating empowering new beliefs. I don't spend time each day/week being creative, or reflecting on how to create an *extraordinary* business. I haven't discovered what I am best at and enjoy doing that is *different* from what my peers are doing and that requires relatively little effort from me.

My Coaching Practice Level:	**VIRTUOSO COACH** I can create clients whenever I choose to.
To reach this level:	**Master the Art of Natural Success:** Remember that success is exponential. Take risks. Stay in the game. And know when to quit.
How to move to the *next* level:	**Be vulnerable:** Practice fearless coaching, which includes hiding nothing from your client. Risk failure.
How to remain at this level:	I am not willing to risk failure by developing and experimenting with new skills or ways of being. I don't have a community of powerful and insightful friends, colleagues, mentors and clients. I don't seek honest and authentic feedback from this community on my unique gifts, my way of being and what holds me back the most. I don't put huge effort into honing my talents, so that it becomes exponentially greater than anyone else's. I am unwilling to risk disapproval.
My Coaching Practice Level:	**MASTER COACH** I can take extended vacations and/or create income whilst I sleep.
To reach this level:	**Master the Art of Freedom:** Live from *Hell Yeah* or *No*.
How to move to the *next* level:	**Never stop learning:** Mastery is the game of a lifetime.
How to remain at this level:	I forget to truly serve others.

Insight: What do I see differently?

_____

_____

Action: What's one tiny step I will take based on this insight?

_____

_____

Insight: What do I see differently?

_____

_____

Action: What's one tiny step I will take based on this insight?

_____

_____

Insight: What do I see differently?

_____

_____

Action: What's one tiny step I will take based on this insight?

_____

_____

The Litvin List

What is the power and impact of YOUR coaching?

Rank each item below from 0 –10

(Where 0 = *I'm nowhere near...* and 10 = *I've nailed it!*)

____ **Outcome Goals**

An outcome goal is bold and audacious and gets me in action. I understand that the only other purpose of an outcome goal is to have me feel amazing in this moment. I have an outcome goal that both excites me and scares me. (*Example:* I call one potential client a day. Or I make three bold requests a week)

____ **Process Goals**

A process goal is clear and achievable in a fixed time period. I have clear process goals for the next ninety days, so that each morning and week after week I know where to focus my time, my energy and my attention. I have habits and rituals that support and renew me on a daily/weekly basis. (*Example:* I call one potential client a day. Or I make three bold requests a week. Or I spend ten minutes planning my day before I check email.)

Mindset

It's okay to feel nervous or scared (that's called being human) but I commit to never let my fears, doubts, limiting beliefs or insecurities hold me back from taking action. I seek support in crafting a set of empowering new beliefs to help me create the next stage of my life.

Skillset

I understand that confidence is a result, not a requirement, and I continually upgrade my coaching skills and my business skills. I have identified any other skills I need, such as public speaking or writing, and I work on them regularly.

Energy

I know what people, places, habits and things *fill* me with energy. And I know what people, places, habits and things *drain* me of energy. I actively remove those energy drainers from my life.

Creativity

I spend time each day/week being creative. I use my creativity in enrolling clients and also in coaching clients. I am turning an ordinary business into an extraordinary business.

The Art of Deep Coaching

I provide exceptional value to clients. I vulnerably lead my clients in the most powerful way possible. I am committed to serving, not pleasing, my clients.

The Art of Creating Clients

I sell the *experience* of coaching, not the *concept*. I create deep, powerful coaching experiences for potential clients. I adopt an attitude of service. I leave conversations in *possibility*, not *affordability*. I grow my practice by invitation and referral only. I love creating clients as much as I love coaching clients.

Getting the Value of Coaching

I have my own coach so I can do the deep inner work needed to see my own blind spots. I know that I can't take my clients any deeper than I have been able to go in my own life. I model for my clients just how much I believe in the power of coaching by paying for my own coaching. I pay my coach more money than I feel comfortable spending.

Being Unique

I have discovered what I am best at and enjoy doing that is different from what my peers are doing and that requires relatively little effort from me. I put huge effort into honing my skillset, so that it becomes extraordinary.

Service

I regularly ask the question: Who can I serve today? I regularly send referrals to colleagues.

Time vs Money

I complete every task I start. I work towards big goals one tiny step at a time. I understand that discretionary time is far more valuable than money.

Integrity

I'm impeccable with my word. I keep my word to myself and others. I clean up immediately when I don't keep my word.

Authenticity

I'm willing to discover, confront, and tell the truth about myself—whenever and wherever I catch myself not being genuine, real, or authentic. I own my inauthenticities with my clients, too.

Committed to Something Bigger than Myself

I am committed to something bigger than myself that allows me to continue in the face of impossible hurdles and barriers. I get that no amount of money, fame, position or power will ever be enough. And I understand that life brings true joy when I am used for a purpose that I know is a mighty one.

Thought Leadership/Influence

I make my unique talents more unusual and more impactful every year. I build a body of work. I develop intellectual property that I share to help others use these skills. I am willing to risk disapproval in sharing my unorthodox way of seeing the world.

How to fearlessly create a powerful coaching conversation

Litvin's client creation formula

Step 1. Connect

How much time did you spend building/creating relationships with people in the past thirty days? Include things like phoning a colleague or old friend, networking events, dinners, parties workshops, lunches, meeting for coffee, etc. Do not include building an email list, working on a website, time on Facebook, time on email, or writing a blog.

1. Do your research before even a first connection. Look them up on Google, LinkedIn and Facebook. Read their blog, their website or their book.

2. Get into an attitude of service.

3. Bring a sense of humor.

4. Adopt a spirit of curiosity.

5. Just connect. Ask them how they are. Ask about their life, ask about their business, ask about their relationships. Don't get too intense if this is a first conversation, just be genuinely curious.

6. Ask what support they most need. Could you connect them with someone useful? Is there a book you could send them that would be just right for their current challenge?

7. If they ask about you, tell them what you are up to.

8. If this is the first time you have spoken to this person do not be in a rush to move to the next step. Building great relationships takes time. Be prepared to connect with this person many times over the next few months (with a spirit of service) before the time is right to ask the next question.

Step 2. Invite

How many potential clients did you invite to experience a Powerful Coaching Conversation with you in the past thirty days?

Be a professional coach, not a social one.

1. Even if you think you are speaking to a "dream client," begin your question with the words, "Who do you know...?" Then get real specific. For example, if you coach women entrepreneurs who have run at least one successful business, you could say, "I have a space for one client right now and I only take on new clients by referral from people I trust. So *who do you know* who is an entrepreneur with a proven track record of success—but who is at this moment facing the challenge of transitioning to a new business?"

2. Then PAUSE... Bite your tongue if you need to. Give them space to think for a moment. If you've described their situation accurately, often the next words will be: "That's me!"

3. "That's me! How much do you charge?" If this is the response, resist the temptation to answer the question. Instead say, "Actually, my coaching is tailor-made. And I don't even know if you really need long-term coaching right now. Instead let me block out two hours for you at a beautiful location, or even over the phone. Experience powerful life-changing coaching. At the end of the two hours you might be complete and not even need any more coaching. And *if* you'd like to know more at that point, and *if* it feels like a fit to *both* of us, we'll talk."

4. Then pull out your calendar and agree on a date and venue there and then.

5. "You should speak to so-and-so..." If this is the response (instead of "that's me!"), resist the temptation to say, "Awesome! Give me her number, I'll call her." Instead slow down the conversation. Take your time to ask the following questions: "Thanks so much for the referral. Tell me, why do you think she would want coaching? Has she ever had coaching before? What's her biggest gift? What's her biggest challenge right now? How do you think coaching will benefit her most? How do you think she will respond if you tell her about coaching?"

6. If after all this it feels like a good fit, explain, "I want you to know that I never cold-call. But if you think she would get value from spending time with me, I will block out two hours with her. And please tell her that I am willing to do this as a gift, to her from you. Have her call or email me and say that she was referred by you. Will you do that?"

Step 3. Create (Your Magic)

How many potential clients did you spend time with in a powerful coaching conversation in the past thirty days? It only counts if you asked—*and received*—permission to coach them. Do not include time coaching a friend, colleague or family member where you were having a chat that turned into coaching. That is not the

Serve them so powerfully they never forget your conversation for the rest of their life.

same as a powerful coaching experience. This is where you get to do *your* magic. Show up powerfully. Dig deep to discover what they really, really want. Hold nothing back. Give them the best coaching experience they have ever had. Look for what they cannot see. And be bold enough to say to them what no one else will say.

Step 4. Propose (and Direct)

How much money did you make in Proposals in the past thirty days? A proposal is where you explicitly say to a person, "It will cost $X to work with me for Y months." It's a proposal when you find out what would be a *Hell Yeah!* for a potential client. It's a proposal when you

"Are you in? HELL YEAH! or no?"

ask them: *Hell Yeah! or No?* It's a proposal when you say, "This is how you make your payment. We begin the moment you send the money."

1. Once again, don't be in a rush. Making a proposal when you are creating a high-paying, high-performing client can require a depth of experience and relationship-building between the two of you over a significant period of time. I have seen this take over two years in some cases.

2. If you have got to the end of the coaching session and they have had a powerful insight or breakthrough, sometimes the very best thing to do is to sit in absolute silence and wait for them to speak first. If you have really rocked their world, this can last from five to thirty minutes. Say nothing.

3. If the silence has lasted long enough or they say, "Thank you" or "What next?" then you can say, "Would you like to hear a little bit about what it could look like for us to work together?" Remember, you cannot rush this. You are not selling a fifteen-dollar book; you are selling high-end coaching.

4. If they are ready to hear more, you can use The Litvin List above to craft a coaching program for them. Pick around five of the items and then relate them specifically to their challenges or goals. For example, "You want to transition smoothly to the role of CEO, so the first part of our work together will be to remove the fears, doubts and insecurities that are holding you back. Secondly, we will craft powerful goals that allow you to inspire and motivate your team. Next, we will review how you manage your energy from day to day. And finally we will help you build ways to ensure your relationship with your husband thrives in the midst of this new challenge. How does that sound to you? What else would we need to add to make this exactly the coaching program you are looking for?"

5. If you are relatively new to enrolling high-end clients then you *must* decide on your numbers well before this conversation begins. If you are experienced at this, you can make your numbers up on the spot, based on the program you are willing to offer.

Here are some examples of ways to make a proposal:

"Your investment will be $55,000 for a year of coaching. You pay up front and there are no refunds."

"It's $30,000 to work with me for a year. But I am not offering that to you. Instead, I would like to create a ninety-day program for you. It is an $8,000 investment. If at the end of this time we both wish to continue, we will talk."

"I charge $12,000 for six months of coaching. But that's not what you need right now. Instead, let's get together for a full day. You will bring along your challenges and we will handle as many as we can in that day-long session. It's $1,500 for the day. And I will include a follow-up coaching session by phone, one week later."

6. Please, please, please practice saying your numbers out loud before the session. Say them to your husband. Say them to your kids. Say them to yourself in the bathroom mirror. But practice saying them out loud so much that they begin to roll off your tongue like your phone number.

7. When you have made your proposal, once again: slow down...

8. If they say they are in, *challenge their "yes."* I know, it seems counterintuitive. But this is how you will create the most committed clients on the planet. "Are you sure I am not rushing you? Do you need to speak to your husband/wife first? This is an important decision; do you want to take some time to reflect?"

9. Then, this is how you complete a powerful proposal. Tell them:

    "This is what I require of you if you wish to work with me. You need to agree that you will never let fear get in the way of you taking action. It's okay to feel fear—that's called being human. You just won't let it get in the way. You need to commit to being authentic with me and hiding nothing. And you need to agree to make all payments as agreed, no exceptions."

"So let's put a date on our calendar right now for when we speak next. That will become our first coaching session once you have signed up."

"You are in once you send a check to me at this address... Or let me take your VISA card number."

Tracking sheet

Every week my clients email me with the answers to four questions:

1. **Connect:** How many people did you connect with this week? (Write out their names.)

2. **Invite:** How many people did you invite to a powerful coaching conversation with you this week? (Write out their names.)

3. **Create (Your Magic):** How many people did you give a powerful experience of your coaching? (Write out their names.)

4. **Propose:** How much money did you propose for coaching engagements this week? (Write out the number in dollars.)

If you track these, over time you will build a thriving coaching practice. Use the worksheets on the following pages to help your tracking for the next month. What gets measured gets done.

Week 1

Connect: How many people did you connect with this week? (Write out their names).

_____

_____

_____

Invite: How many people did you invite to a powerful coaching conversation with you this week? (Write out their names).

_____

_____

Create (Your Magic): How many people did you give a powerful experience of your coaching? (Write out their names).

_____

_____

Propose: How much money did you propose for coaching engagements this week? (Write out the number in dollars).

_____

Week 2

Connect: How many people did you connect with this week? (Write out their names).

_____

_____

_____

Invite: How many people did you invite to a powerful coaching conversation with you this week? (Write out their names).

_____

_____

Create (Your Magic): How many people did you give a powerful experience of your coaching? (Write out their names).

_____

_____

Propose: How much money did you propose for coaching engagements this week? (Write out the number in dollars).

_____

Week 3

Connect: How many people did you connect with this week? (Write out their names).

_____

_____

_____

Invite: How many people did you invite to a powerful coaching conversation with you this week? (Write out their names).

_____

_____

Create (Your Magic): How many people did you give a powerful experience of your coaching? (Write out their names).

_____

_____

Propose: How much money did you propose for coaching engagements this week? (Write out the number in dollars).

_____

Week 4

Connect: How many people did you connect with this week? (Write out their names).

_____

_____

_____

Invite: How many people did you invite to a powerful coaching conversation with you this week? (Write out their names).

_____

_____

Create (Your Magic): How many people did you give a powerful experience of your coaching? (Write out their names).

_____

_____

Propose: How much money did you propose for coaching engagements this week? (Write out the number in dollars).

_____

The NO game

THERE COMES A MOMENT when I set almost every one of my clients who is a coach or consultant the same assignment: Your mission—if you choose to accept it—is to see how many *no's* you can collect in the next seven days. How many potential clients can you get to say *no* to you in the next week?

Most coaches feel so rejected by the *no's* that they stop asking. Playing the NO game and having your only goal to see how many potential clients can say *no* to you changes everything. Suddenly coaches are excited to make proposals and to say big numbers out loud.

Make your measure of success the number of *no's* you collect each day. As Byron Katie says: "You can have *anything* you want in life, if you are willing to ask a thousand people..."

Fear and excuses

Here's how you handle some of the most common thoughts that stand in the way of succeeding as a coach.

They can't afford it.

You have no idea what they can afford. Stop making up stories. I have seen people say they can't afford coaching and then go on holiday for three weeks. Give them the best coaching experience they have ever had and let them choose where they will invest their money.

I'm not worth that much.

Your "worth" is irrelevant. Coaching changes lives. And their dreams are priceless. Put all your attention on the value they will get from coaching.

I don't know how to set fees.

Pick a number. Raising your rates is the easiest thing in the world. For now, pick a number, preferably two. And practice saying it out loud until it rolls off your tongue like your phone number.

I don't know who to speak to.

Call an old friend. Call a colleague. Go to a social event. And put yourself in a service mindset. Give instead of take.

I need a client.

If you can't pay the rent you don't need a client, you need a job. Forget coaching. Find a way to create income immediately. You will never create high-end clients from a needy place. Once your basic expenses are covered and you no longer 'need' a client you are in a perfect position to start coaching again.

I can't afford my own coach.

If you don't believe enough in coaching to invest in your own coach, why would anyone ever invest in you? Find a way to save what you need for the very best coach you can afford. Model what it takes to your own clients.

I keep getting *no's.*

Awesome! Play the NO game (see Appendix 5). But if you only ever get *no's*, it either means your coaching is not powerful enough or you are in too much of a rush. Creating high—paying clients cannot be rushed.

I don't know how to get into the corporate world.

Start with what you know. You have a background in accounting, law, marketing—then seek out the people you know because you know their secret dreams and their secret fears better than anyone.

Questions & Answers

with Steve and Rich

QUESTION #1:

How would you handle a last-minute cancellation when you've blocked out two hours for a prospective client? Today I had a scheduled coaching session and just six minutes before the start time I received this text message from my client:

> *Something came up I need to reschedule our apt for today sorry*

RICH:

Start by reflecting on this from the inside-out. Ask yourself some high flame questions. Who would you have to *be* as a coach to have a client cancel at the last minute, by text message?

I put commitment front and center of any conversation I have with a potential client. I let them know what I am committed to. And I make really clear the kind of commitments I require in my clients.

You see, money is only one sign of commitment. My clients need to commit far more than just money to work with me. They need to commit time and energy and drive and focus. And more. They need to commit to taking action (even if they are afraid). They need to commit to being their word—or cleaning up (although they never need to apologize to me, for anything). They need to commit to being on time. And they need to commit to calling themselves out where they are out of integrity.

In the very first session with every new client, I spend up to two hours crafting clear and personalized Agreements. And, I have every new client listen to Steve Chandler's audio called *Expectation vs Agreement*. So we create a world—from the very first time we work together—where they understand the power of clear agreements.

No one has to create your clients the way I do. But what is certain is that *how* your clients show up is a factor of how *you* create them.

• • •

Okay. Now having done your own Deep Inner Work, consider apologizing to your client. Sounds counterintuitive, right?

Apologize for not serving her the best way you could as her coach. Apologize for not introducing her to the concept of Agreements vs Expectations. Apologize to her for not showing up in the most powerful way you could. And then let her know that you won't ever let her down like that again.

Craft really strong, clear agreements for the rest of your time coaching together. Offer her an extra session if you need to. Go deep. And ask her: where else in your life do you not have clear agreements? With your husband? Your kids? Your boss? Your employees? Your team? After all, "How we do 'anything' is how we do 'everything.'"

This could be the most impactful coaching she ever receives, if you are willing to take her there. But begin from a vulnerable place by owning your own mistakes.

QUESTION #2:

I met a potential client who emailed me to ask if we might set up a time for a "get acquainted" talk on the phone. I suggested a time and his response was, "I'm probably available. Click this link and go to my online calendar, and if that time is open, schedule our conversation."

His online calendar (which showed a lot of openings) took me to a sign-up page. I was completely put off. Any suggestions as to what I could do next?

RICH:

This is classic *Role Reversal*: the attempt by a potential client to set the terms for how their coach will show up. The alternative is the *Fearless Coaching* approach: the willingness of the coach to be the boldest person in the room. At a moment like this, most coaches show up as needy and willing to do anything to please a potential client. Don't do that. *You* are the valuable resource here. Help them to see that.

STEVE:

"Hey, I don't want to get acquainted. I don't want a new friend. I don't want to get to know you. My work consists of helping people create wealth. Do you need help in that area or are you okay? If you need help, call me Tuesday at 10 EST and I will help you."

QUESTION #3:

A client just cancelled five months of upcoming sessions, saying that she was happy with how our work had turned her life around and that she didn't need more coaching for now.

She signed up for six months of coaching, but she's fine with letting it go. So I'd appreciate ideas on how to encourage someone in this situation to open up to the possibility that there may be even greater breakthroughs down the line. Any suggestions?

STEVE:

It isn't about *encouraging* her or persuading her or finessing her or manipulating her. That's the old *sales model* of coaching-practice building that fails (but only always). It is about listening to her.

This client is like the person who cancels her gym membership because she's "strong enough" already. You know she is covering for something. The question is whether I can find it in our final session. If so, I can help her with what she's too afraid to bring up. I want to do a session that breaks all the rules and uncovers the thought that has kicked her out of heaven.

QUESTION #4:

Do you have experience coaching business owners in the IT industry? I was attempting to help a client with a big account that is a few months late in paying. He insists that in the IT industry there is a thirty-day window for an invoice getting paid and companies often pay late. He says this is how the IT industry works. Do you have any experience in coaching someone in the IT industry that would be useful for me to know in helping him to solve his problem?

RICH:

Refuse to buy into his story. Refuse to speak to *anyone* else in his industry. He doesn't need another person who believes the story he already thinks is true. Challenge his way of seeing the world. It's the biggest gift you could ever give him.

QUESTION #5:

My friends often ask me to coach them for free, or to exchange our services. What do you do in that situation?

RICH:

Yesterday, someone I know reached out to me with a request for coaching at no charge. He wanted to offer me Search Engine Optimization support in return. Here is my reply:

I am willing to support you. It will not be how you imagine. I am a coach. I am a powerful coach. For this reason I never coach for free. For you I am willing to make an exception. For a single powerful session. However, this is what I require of you if you wish to receive my support.

My support will be to serve you, not to please you. My coaching is high flame. In our conversations, I will not be your friend. I will be your coach. I will say things to you that no one else will say. I will hold nothing back.

Our conversations will be professional. Not social. We will not discuss our kids, our relationships or our lives (except where they are directly relevant to your coaching). Everything we discuss I will keep confidential from people we know.

Before we speak, answer the questions below and email me your answers.

And if this doesn't feel like a fit, please call it a clear no.

My coaching is not for everyone.

QUESTION #6:

There are a ton of misconceptions in our field and the vast majority of new coaches never make it. What's the number one reason why most coaches fail? And what's the number one key to success as a coach?

STEVE:

The Key to Failure: taking yourself seriously. The Key to Success: taking your work seriously.

YOU ARE NOT
ALONE

A note from Rich

I'VE ALWAYS LOVED ADVENTURES. As a kid, I was an avid reader of adventure stories. And I camped across England, Wales and Scotland as a boy scout. I hitchhiked around Israel when I was seventeen. I traveled alone around India at twenty-one. I taught science in a rural school in Botswana at twenty-four. And I was once given a diamond-encrusted watch by the world's wealthiest man.

I love to tell stories about my adventures (just ask my wife). But the truth is I have a very selective memory.

And like me, some of your best stories are probably about your most challenging moments. I have been robbed at knife-point. I was once so sick in Calcutta that I couldn't move for four days. Another time I was terrified when charged by a rhino—to make it worse I was on horseback at the time and barely knew how to ride. Once I saved the life of a man about to be killed for stealing in an African village!

These days I am pretty good at making these sound like cool stories, but the truth is that over the course of my travels I've been sick and I've been scared and I've felt very alone.

In the years since I began coaching as a full-time career I have had some incredible successes and helped my clients do some amazing things. I've learned to create a coaching practice by invitation and referral only, with a few powerful, high-end clients. And I've helped many other coaches do the same.

So I have some great stories to share about how to create high-paying clients, but the truth is that—just like on my travels—along the way I've been sick and I've been scared and I've felt very alone.

So if you ever feel upset or sad or scared that you won't be able to succeed as a coach, or that one day the magic will run out and the dream will fall apart, you are not alone.

Join us at TheProsperousCoach.com to explore how we can support you and how we can connect you with our amazing community of coaches.

About the Authors

Rich Litvin lives his life based on one principle: *Hell Yeah! or No.* He is one of the world's most exclusive success coaches and his clients are by invitation and referral only. He has worked with CEOs, millionaires, Olympic athletes, celebrities, best-selling authors, soldiers, mothers and other coaches.

An expert on deep, lasting, natural confidence, Litvin specializes in helping high achieving introverts identify the blocks that keep them from attaining even greater levels of accomplishment. His clients are powerful, passionate, and prosperous, with a track record of success. They work with Litvin because they are ready for their next level of success.

A scientist by training, Litvin has a background in Behavioral Physiology and Psychology. He trained to teach at the University of Oxford and he has a master's degree in Educational Effectiveness.

Litvin is the founder and CEO of the Confident Woman's Salon, where he works with some of the world's most successful women. A thought leader in the coaching world, he is a member of the Association of Transformational Leaders. He has served as the CEO of a coaching organization and on the faculty of two coach training schools. His clients who are coaches or consultants already make six figures, or have had a high level of success in another field.

Litvin has lived and worked in eight countries and on four continents. A former teacher and leader of one of the most challenging inner-city schools in London, his students have ranged from children in rural African villages to the son of the world's wealthiest man. His wife, Monique, is an award-winning singer/songwriter. They are the proud parents of a baby boy named Kaleo. And Litvin still gets nervous walking into a party.

Litvin spends his time between Los Angeles and London and can be reached at www.RichLitvin.com.

Steve Chandler is a world-famous personal success coach to people from all walks of life, including best-selling authors, public speakers, CEOs and media personalities, small business owners, university faculty and leaders, major account salespeople and the world's top business and life coaches.

As a corporate trainer he has worked with over thirty Fortune 500 companies and more than 600 other organizations in the areas of goal achievement, ownership culture, and sales and leadership. He has also served as a fundraising consultant and trainer to non-profits and is the co-author of the best-selling *RelationShift: Revolutionary Fundraising*.

Chandler is also a nationally recognized keynote speaker with over 1,000 speeches given throughout the U.S. and Canada. He is the creator and leader of two year-long Steve Chandler Mastermind groups and five Steve Chandler Coaching Schools for top-level business coaches, marketing consultants and life coaches. He has also served as a visiting teacher and lecturer at the University of Santa Monica graduate program in Soul-Centered Leadership and as a special guest coach on the award-winning TV reality program *Starting Over*.

Chandler is the author and co-author of dozens of books, including the bestsellers, *Time Warrior, 100 Ways to Motivate Yourself, Reinventing Yourself, 100 Ways to Motivate Others, 17 Lies That Are Holding You Back* and *Fearless*. His books have been translated into more than forty foreign-language editions. He is the creator and writer of the popular blog www.imindshift.com.

Chandler is a graduate of both the University of Arizona (Creative Writing and Political Science) and the elite Defense Language Institute, Presidio of Monterey, California (Russian language). He is a Cold War veteran, with four years of military service at the U.S. Army Security Agency in Berlin, Germany, and Psychological Warfare at Fort Bragg, North Carolina.

Chandler lives outside of Phoenix, Arizona, and can be reached at www.SteveChandler.com.

Acknowledgments

Steve acknowledges:

Kathy Eimers

Rich Litvin

Steve Hardison

Mary Hulnick

Michelle Bauman

Ron Hulnick

Matt Furey

Michael Neill

Sam Beckford

Stephen McGhee

Ken Wilber

Carolyn Freyer–Jones

Werner Erhard

Dusan Djukich

Byron Katie

Sherry Phelan

Chris Dorris

Nathaniel Branden

Rich acknowledges:

I have had the fortune to have worked with—and become friends with—some of the most gifted coaches and teachers on the planet.

Steve Chandler, I could not have done this without you. You inspire me. And you challenge the hell out of me. It has been an honor and a privilege to share this journey with you. I am proud to be able to call you my coach, my mentor and my friend.

Michael Neill, I am indebted to you for your guidance, support and love. I'll never forget the moment when I was considering signing up with you but I was terrified to invest so much money. You said, "I could coach you on that. But I think it's a distraction. Because somewhere deep down inside you know. You either want to work with me. Or you don't." And you were so right. And I did know. And they always know.

Steve Hardison, you helped me kill the chameleon. You helped me bring back Richard The Lionheart. You helped me create my world. I am eternally grateful.

Decker Cunov, you let me keep showing up and showing up. I was honored to be part of the team for a short while. You are one of the most intuitive coaches I know. You helped me understand the true power of authenticity. And I love you.

Nicole Daedone, you saw something in a nervous British guy that I could not see in myself and you were willing to set the bar high for me and accept nothing less. You taught me more about myself than anyone I have ever had the privilege of spending time with. You are never afraid to push into my edges and show me that the world isn't how I think it is. There's more to come.

Kevin O'Malley, you modeled for me the power of vulnerability. I showed up with a story that I didn't need coaching. You saw through that story and cracked me open. And my life has never been the same. You changed my world.

Guy Sengstock and **Alexis Shepperd**, you showed me how to truly "get" a client's world, from the inside-out. Most coaches have no idea how this is done. You both live from that place.

Jerry Candelaria, you truly "got" my world, from the inside-out.

Clarence Thompson, you introduced me to the Enneagram and showed me a path to real freedom. You are the only seventy-something, ex-priest, successful businessman, teacher, musician and meta-coach I know. And I am thrilled whenever I have an opportunity to spend time with you or send a client in your direction.

Peleg Top, your passion for design, your love of beauty, your willingness to seek—and walk—your own path in life inspire me. I was fortunate to have met you just as I arrived in Los Angeles.

Nicolas Sage, John Wineland, Mark Thornton, Teo Alfero, Keith Kegley: It's been a privilege to have shared such a powerful journey with you. Thank you for never buying into my story, for keeping me grounded and for challenging me to lean into my edge. But only always.

Sam Horn, you motivate me with your vision, your ability to create community and your way of seeing the world so clearly that I am inspired to take action on every occasion I am fortunate enough to spend time with you.

Alan Weiss, you are a rock star in my world. Value-based fees changed everything for me. Million Dollar Coaching set my bar high. And your willingness to be a contrarian helped me begin creating my own body of work.

Jamie Smart, you couldn't have known it at the time but your coaching cards helped me begin my career on that beach in Thailand. Six years later and you've become one of my best friends in the world. I am grateful for the time we spend together eating Thai food.

Sean Stephenson, there are few men in the world I trust absolutely. You are one of them. Hanging out, together or with our wives is always a highlight of my calendar.

Brian Whetten, thank you for seeing me. Thank you for trusting me. Thank you for sharing the journey with me.

Stever Robbins, your guidance and support on the journey of writing this book has been invaluable.

Chris Nelson, you are an extraordinary editor with such an eye for detail. **Danielle Baird**, I am thrilled to have you as the designer on my team. Your work is exemplary. **David Michael Moore**, you demonstrated that a picture is worth a thousand words.

Christine Livingston, Eirik Grunde Olsen, Jasmine Keel, Kelly Ramon, Megan Sillito, Nadjeschda Taranczewski, Terrance Thames, Vanessa Horn.

Monique DeBose, I proposed before I'd even heard your amazing voice. You are a beautiful, loving presence. You bring the music and the magic into my world. And I love you.

Kaleo Rex Theodore Litvin, at just eighteen months old you are my favorite teacher in the whole wide world. I love you.

High-Achieving Introverts:

Unleash the Power of Your Quiet Top Performers.

Up to fifty percent of the people we know are introverts. My current research and coaching focus on introverts who are already high achievers or who aspire to be. Women who are first time CEOs. Women who are successful entrepreneurs balancing their business with raising a family. Entrepreneurs and employees in Fortune 500 tech and media companies. Bloggers, writers, social media and traditional media experts who thrive working alone.

High-achieving introverts regularly accomplish goals that feel easy to them but which astound their peers. They aren't interested in following the crowd and don't like small talk. They understand the power of being alone, are deeply reflective and are willing to take risks—but only to make a big impact in the world. They perform at high levels with little guidance or support. Yet they can feel like a fraud because their career is thriving whilst their relationships suffer. They can make a great deal of money but not have enough time with their family. They can be well known in their area of expertise but drained by the challenges of living a high-energy life. They may feel like they are hiding a secret that no one around them can understand because they are frustrated by the sense that there is so much more possible for them.

These quiet top performers are leading, achieving or creating an impact in the world not *despite* their introversion but *because* of it. When entrepreneurs, CEOs and organizations harness the full power of their introverted high achievers the results can be exponential. Greater autonomy, mastery and purpose. Increased resilience, creativity and natural motivation. And ultimately a big impact on the personal and corporate bottom line.

An introverted high achiever myself and founder of the Confident Woman's Salon, I have coached and interviewed some of the world's highest achievers—Olympic athletes, millionaires, soldiers, CEOs and celebrities. Powerful, passionate and prosperous individuals with a track record of success. One of the greatest challenges facing high achievers is that they perform at a level which is so high that most people cannot even see how much they are holding back. And top performers have few people in their world willing to say what they most need to hear. Yet tiny changes can account for radical differences in achievement and they have the highest impact for people already achieving and creating close to or at world-class levels. In this rarified atmosphere, the very qualities that have led to their current success are also precisely what hold them back from even greater levels of accomplishment.

Super successful introverts often dream so big that they get overwhelmed. Despite the admiration of those around them, it often doesn't feel like they've ever had to work that hard for everything they've accomplished. And as they play a bigger and bigger game, deeper competing beliefs begin to rise that create an upper limit to their success. High achievers also get comfortable in the 'gray zone'—a working pace that appears impressive but actually leads to a decline in performance. The danger for a high performer is that their 'gray zone' creates so much more than the average person that there is a temptation to continually underperform without even realizing that they are doing so.

Quiet top performers are also extremely talented problem-solvers with a finely-tuned ability to scan the horizon for "danger". They are energized by challenges and threats, so they tend to avoid things—taxes, relationships, income, etc.—until they reach problem-level status. And they seek perfection, so the barrier to start each subsequent project becomes unbearably high because each time it is re-set, based upon the rewards of their previous project.

If you are a Quiet Top Performer who is ready to make a bigger impact and get to your next level, an organization interested in harnessing the full power of your introverted high achievers, or you are simply interested in learning more about my work, please contact me directly: rich@richlitvin.com.

The Wealth Warrior Movement

Serve the world with what you love to do

IN HIS RECENT BOOK, *Wealth Warrior*, Steve related his personal turnaround story: from underachievement, alcoholism, bankruptcy and shame to success, creative action and prosperity. In short, from wealth worrier to wealth warrior. Then, in the spirit of "If I can do this anybody can," he shared inspirations that transformed his life—and showed how to put them into action.

Now Steve has created the Wealth Warrior Movement to enrich the message of the book. Through wealth tips, ongoing inspirations, and live webinars with Steve and special guests, he helps you cultivate a transformative warrior mindset. It is a program designed not just to help you create more wealth, but to truly prosper in all areas of your life.

As Steve says, "You and I, operating as creative, inspired individuals, can create the turnaround the world longs for. This yearning for new wealth will be satisfied one person at a time; one inspired individual at a time. I invite you to join this Wealth Warrior Movement and make it your conscious, active purpose to prosper and be a role model for others."

Go to www.SteveChandler.com to register and access the ten-part Creating Wealth audio series.

Email Maurice Bassett at MauriceBassett@gmail.com for a sample audio program.

Books by Steve Chandler

Wealth Warrior

Time Warrior

The Life Coaching Connection

Fearless

The Woman Who Attracted Money

Shift Your Mind Shift the World

17 Lies That Are Holding You Back

10 Commitments to Your Success

Reinventing Yourself

The Story of You

100 Ways to Motivate Yourself

How to Get Clients

50 Ways to Create Great Relationships

The Joy of Selling

RelationShift (with Michael Bassoff)

The Small Business Millionaire (with Sam Beckford)

100 Ways to Create Wealth (with Sam Beckford)

9 Lies That Are Holding Your Business Back (with Sam Beckford)

Business Coaching (with Sam Beckford)

100 Ways to Motivate Others (with Scott Richardson)

The Hands Off Manager (with Duane Black)

Two Guys On the Road (with Terrence Hill)

Two Guys Read the Box Scores (with Terrence Hill)

Two Guys Read Jane Austen (with Terrence Hill)

Two Guys Read Moby Dick (with Terrence Hill)

Two Guys Read the Obituaries (with Terrence Hill)

Powerful Graceful Success

Audios by Steve Chandler

MindShift: The Steve Chandler Success Course

Time Warrior

9 Lies That Are Holding Your Business Back

10 Habits of Successful Salespeople

17 Sales Lies

Are You A Doer Or A Feeler?

Challenges

Choosing

Creating Clients: Referrals

Creating Clients: The 18 Disciplines

Creative Relationships

Expectation vs. Agreement

Financially Fearless

How To Double Your Income As A Coach

How To Help A Pessimist

How To Solve Problems

Information vs. Transformation

Is It A Dream Or A Project?

Making A Difference

Ownership And Leadership

People People

Personality Reinvented

Purpose vs. Personality

Serving vs. Pleasing People

Testing vs. Trusting

The Fearless Mindset

Life really can be
exponential.

You are far closer
to everything you
want than you could
ever imagine.

Miracles are far
closer than you think.